PRAISE FOR

IN LIFE SCHOOL

"Recently I have gone through the life experiences of cancer, divorce, and the loss of my home. During these times, so many people asked me how I kept such a positive and peaceful attitude. My answer is my daily reading of the inspirational wisdom within Rob's book."

Tammy Clifton, Interior Designer

"Seldom has there been such a unique compilation of inspirational truth presented in a straightforward manner that explores the subjects of happiness, gratitude, forgiveness, and creating a better life today."

Gaylord Bolduc, Mental Health Counselor

"Rob's book is filled with authentic inspiration and uplifting words that will elevate your soul."

Kim Somers Egelsee, Author of *Getting Your Life to a Ten Plus*

"I work in a hospital and I have posted many of *In Life School's* writings on our Positivity Board. This book has benefited both those of us who work together and our patients. Thank you, Rob, for opening our eyes to the possibilities of life and helping us to be better people."

Margie Rasmussen, Hospital Employee

"There have been so many times that the words of Rob's book have touched my life, by delivering wisdom, love, and healing."

Gwen Lepard, *Joyful Living Radio*

"I believe that we learn through life's lessons. Rob Whalley's book is a life coaching tool. I have learned a lot and you will too."

Katie Richardson, Life Coach

"When I hit the lowest point in my life, Rob's book helped me turn my problems into possibilities. His words helped me find a new outlook on life by teaching me to be at peace with my past and hopeful for the future. It is the best self-help book I have ever read."

Ramandeep Singh Kukreja, Dentist

"Mr. Whalley's writings are from the heart and are full of wisdom and inspiration. I will definitely keep a copy for all of my Bed and Breakfast guests to read."

Ann Harwood, Bear Spirit Lodge

"After we lost our house, I would slip into a state of feeling sorry for myself. That's when Rob's messages of inspiration would put me right back into a positive mode again!"

Debbie McGowan, Contractor

"Rob's book makes a simple but powerful point: throughout our lives we are always in school, and we always have one more lesson to learn *In Life School.*"

Tyler R. Tichelaar, Author of *Narrow Lives*

"I am a victim of a violent crime, and through the wisdom and guidance in this book, I am learning how to forgive the past, love myself again, and move forward."

Debbie Talley, Bookkeeper

"As a recent divorcee, I spent a lot of time questioning things about my life. Rob's writings helped me take better actions, and become a happy person again!"

Jimmy Robbins, Salesman

"*In Life School* is a heart-centered book filled with wisdom. I recommend you take the time to read this wonder-full book."

Debra Oakland, Blog Writer

"The words I read in Rob's book have helped change my negative thought-patterns into positive ones."

Donna Watkins, Customer Service Rep.

"We all have times in our lives when we don't quite know which road to take. Rob Whalley's inspirational messages have often been a guide."

Pamela Capone Mason, Grocery Manager

"I have thoroughly enjoyed these wise and powerful words that speak to the highest aspects of our spiritual and human nature."

Callie K. Byron, Mental Health Therapist

"This book has helped me surrender to life's hurdles and to seek the lessons in my daily life experiences."

Greg Chastain, Pastor

"Rob Whalley's book has helped me to really live! I now accept my past, and I forgive myself for the first time in my fifty-eight years of living."

"Rob's book has touched me in my spirit. I am sure Rob's words will aid you in lighting your path in life."

"I use Rob's life-changing book to improve the quality of my daily life. This book helps me look at things with a positive and loving perspective."

"*In Life School* is a pouring forth of lessons learned, given in love, to lift and inspire us all."

"At the time I found Rob's book, I had fallen into a dark place of clinical depression. Daily, I would read Rob's words where I found renewed hope through the healing and light in his book."

"*In Life School*, shows us that it isn't what happens to us, but how we react to what happens to us, that determines our destiny in life."

"*In Life School* is where you learn your greatest lessons. This book will become one of your all time favorites."

"I am so grateful every time I receive a life lesson from Rob's book."

Juniper Mainelis, Entertainer

"I rely upon Rob's uplifting words of wisdom for guidance and strength each day. Thanks for being there beside me through the pages of your book."

Cathy Edwards, Business Owner

"Rob's words have helped me heal toward a more loving heart and better health of mind, body, and spirit."

Annie Papazian, Photographer

"All of your writings help me live life to the fullest and teach me to enjoy the ride, regardless of the bumps in the road."

Barbara Rush, Health Care Provider

"I have shared Rob's book with my friends who are dealing with the trials and challenges of life. I feel his book is a great tool for inspired healing and change."

Mike Garrett, Restaurant Owner

"Rob's writings have often been like a best friend, and I truly enjoy his positive encouragement!"

JoAnna Tupman, Real Estate Specialist

"I am a very positive person, but sometimes I need a push to be more so. The teachings of *In Life School* put me back into a positive frame of mind."

Candace Boone Marteski, Wife & Mother

"I am forever reading the pages in Rob's book. All of the life courses help me on my life's journey."

Bill Young, High School Friend

Your Success Course for Learning Life's Biggest Lessons

IN
LIFE
SCHOOL

Living Is Your Classroom
Experience Is Your Teacher
Loving Is Your Test

ROB WHALLEY

AVIVA
PUBLISHING
New York

IN LIFE SCHOOL

Living is Your Classroom, Experience Is Your Teacher, Loving Is Your Test
Copyright © 2014 Rob Whalley

Address inquiries to:
InLifeSchool@gmail.com
www.InLifeSchool.com
www.facebook.com/rob.whalley.9
www.facebook.com/inlifeschool
www.twitter.com/InLifeSchool

ISBN: 978-1-940984-43-8
Library of Congress Control Number: 2014945837

Editor: Tyler Tichelaar, www.MarquetteFiction.com
Book Coach: Patrick Snow, www.ThePublishingDoctor.com
Cover & Interior Design: Fusion Creative Works, www.fusioncw.com

Printed in the United States of America
First Edition
For additional copies visit: www.InLifeSchool.com

Published by
Aviva Publishing
Lake Placid, NY
518.523.1320
www.AvivaPubs.com

DEDICATION

To Pam...

You will always be my best friend and I hold a place for you in my heart. Thank you for living a loving and wisdom-filled life that inspired the writing of my song "Everything Happens for a Reason," which in turn became the inspiration for writing this book. Your journey to the other side encouraged me to find the strength and faith to believe in my vision of writing and finishing this book.

To My Readers…

Thank you for investing your time and money into reading my book. I believe with all of my heart, mind, and soul that you will benefit greatly from everything you will read and learn during our time spent together inside these pages. Everything happens for a reason, including why you are reading *In Life School*. I look forward to meeting you in person some day and sharing our life experiences and lessons. Always remember that "Life is great and getting better every day." See you on Facebook, Twitter, and on my website, InLifeSchool.com. Enjoy the book. Have a best and blessed life today.

CONTENTS

Life School Master's Degree Program

INTRODUCTION

The idea for writing this book came to me almost seven years ago after writing a song about helping my best friend Pam go through her difficult journey with cancer. The song is titled "Everything Happens For A Reason," and I decided to go into the studio and record it. When I shared the idea with a good friend, she suggested that instead of doing another music project, I should write a book. My response was, "Write a book? I don't know how to do that!"

Over time, the idea of writing a book began to grow on me. So for the next several years, I read books and attended book writing seminars in order to learn how to compose and publish a book. I was then very fortunate to meet and employ Patrick Snow as my book writing coach, while he was giving a book publishing seminar in Maui, Hawaii.

I then got the great idea to begin writing my book online by posting my daily book writings on my Facebook page along with inspirational photos. I did this six to ten times a day, and soon I had 5000 friends and over 4000 followers. I literally wrote this book on Facebook. My book, *In Life School*, is the compilation of over three years of writing and posting my words on Facebook.

The theme of this book is that life is a school, based on the learning philosophies that life is your classroom, experience is your teacher, and loving is your test. I will repeatedly be asking you the question, "What have you learned in life and how are you applying those lessons toward living a better life today?" Learning your lessons *IN LIFE SCHOOL* will teach you things you were not taught in the traditional educational system. In this book, I have given you a wealth of knowledge you can teach yourself. I am giving you an opportunity to take the "Change your life for the better challenge" by living and doing what you will read in this insightful book.

This book contains over 300 inspirational quotes by self-help authors, philosophers, famous people, ancient masters, current teachers, and historical figures, who have taught the lessons they learned in life school, including: Socrates, Og Mandino, James Allen, Confucius, Einstein, Eckhart Tolle, Andy Andrews, John Lennon, Dr. Wayne Dyer, Aristotle, Helen Keller, Julius Caesar, Emerson, Thoreau, Dr. Seuss, Deepak Chopra, Jesus, Buddha, Brian Tracy, Norman Vincent Peale, Joel Osteen, Gandhi, Napoleon Hill, Tony Robbins, The Dalai Lama, Zig Ziglar, Dale Carnegie, Abraham Lincoln, Marianne Williamson, Rick Warren, Sigmund Freud, Rumi, Oprah Winfrey, Stephen Covey, and hundreds more wise and successful people. You will also learn through fifty lesson-teaching stories and over forty creeds, poems, and song lyrics. Plus, you will have thirty opportunities to write down your heartfelt answers to the thought-provoking workbook questions.

Inside this book are other people's answers to many of your biggest life questions. Those answers are pieces of your own puzzle that you need to make your life whole. Self-Transformation requires new information, and each page is filled with the wisdom you need. You have to get rid of what isn't working and replace it with what will. There are no mistakes, only lessons, and we all need help with learning the next one.

It is not a coincidence that you have been led to read this book. Our roads in life have intersected and I believe you are going to gain life-changing knowledge from our time spent together inside these inspirational pages. We are all on the same journey, just on different roads. We are all experiencing the same things but with a different heart, mind, and soul. I am just like you, still in the process of learning and applying my life school lessons, even at sixty years young!

I don't have all the answers. For I have failed as much as I have succeeded and lost as much as I have gained. Yet from a very early age, I have been very aware of the importance of learning my lessons in life from my failures and successes, and using them to achieve my best and highest good. I have been very successful at turning the "School of Hard Knocks" into the experience of "Opportunity Knocks." The knowledge contained within *In Life School* will help you acquire the tools and wisdom necessary to be living your best life today.

Learning, changing, and growing is a higher calling into the liberating of the human soul and spirit. I am a vessel that is passing on this knowledge, these truths, and my personal experiences. I believe in the life-changing power of what I have written in this book. Yet only you will know what you need to do in order to be enjoying a greater life experience. Only you can take the right action to change your life for the better. Perhaps this means big changes or some little ones that will make a big difference.

This book is full of simple and easy ways to find solutions for your challenges and give you the self-help to transform bad into good, sickness into healing, depression into happiness, and hate into love. This book is a helping hand for leading you further down the spiritual, emotional, financial, and enlightened path that you are already on. It will bring more light into your life and cast out the darkness that is blinding your vision. I'm talking about real guidance that you can use to improve and change your everyday living experience with healing, renewal, and restoration. You will become stronger, wiser, happier, healthier, and better, as a result of reading and applying the profound spiritual and philosophical truths in this book.

I am not Dr. Rob, or a college professor, yet I have earned a degree from the "University of Life." My life has taught me many lessons through the very educational life experiences of marriage and divorce, happiness and depression, prosperity and loss, friendship and loneliness, love and hate, success and failure, pleasure and pain, and more right and wrong choices than I care to count! I am just a beggar who is hungry, telling another beggar where to find some fresh bread.

The idea is to experience progress, not perfection, from thought to feeling, feeling to action, and action to more positive reactions in your life. What would you give and do to improve your life 10 percent? If you could find a savings account or a CD that would pay you 10 percent interest, you would join the line out the door at the bank to open a new account! If you could be 10 percent healthier, stronger, happier, more loving, and have an overall better life, would you want it?

You can make your life more than 10 percent better by simply making a 1 percent change in your life. At 211 degrees, water is just very hot, yet if you add just 1 degree of heat, the water boils! Because when you change anything, just a little, it is now 100 percent changed from what it used to be. You may not make a touchdown, but you can get close enough to score the winning field goal. I guarantee you that if you read and apply the life principles in this book, your life will be changed for the better today, tomorrow, and into your glorious future. This book will teach you how to say, "Life is great and getting better every day."

I am not saying that as a result of reading this book you will never make another mistake or have a bad day. But I am saying that you will make wiser choices and less mistakes. I am saying that when you have a negative experience, you will not spend as much time being depressed or getting stuck in your problem. Inside this book, you will learn the skills to learn, grow, and prosper while moving forward toward greater understanding. You will enter into a higher place by turning everything into a positive learning opportunity.

My hope is that these life-changing words will deeply touch your heart, mind, and soul. This book includes all of the keys to powerful learning and knowledge: Repetition, writing down your thoughts, affirming and speaking what you want into existence, while being coached by great minds into greater understanding. Each one of these life-changing concepts is a step-up on the ladder that you can use to climb out of where you don't want to be, into the place where you want to be. It took nine months for you to mature from a seed into a newborn baby, so be patient with your growing and changing process.

I am taking this journey with you into living your best life today. So come along with me. "Life School" is now in session. It's time to begin learning the lessons your life wants to teach you… IN LIFE SCHOOL.

Rob Whalley
InLifeSchool.com

COURSE ONE

Living Is Your Classroom

Everyone knows from living his or her life, that there are some things you can only learn through experience. The "Going through your life" teaches you "How to live your life."

> I'm a lover, and a dreamer,
> A wise man, and a fool.
> I'm everything I've ever learned,
> While going through "Life School".

We are all students taking our tests in the classroom of life, through the courses of love, forgiveness, positive thinking, gratitude, overcoming problems, taking action, and making changes. One day at a time, we are learning the lessons we need to live in this world with more power, peace, happiness, and success. We will pass each test and move on to a higher place, when we face life's challenges with a more optimistic and positive attitude.

You are both the student and inspirational teacher of every valuable lesson you will ever learn. You are the daily creator of who you are and what you are becoming, through every thought, feeling, word, and deed. We are all in the process of being taught by everything and everyone, all of the time. Having to repeat the lessons your life wants to teach you is the result of not learning them the first time around! You begin to learn something only when you find the way to teach it to yourself.

"What is the difference between school and life? In school, you are taught a lesson and then given a test. In life, you are given a test that teaches you a lesson."
—Tom Bodett – Radio Host, *The End of the Road*

We are all taking classes in a school called "Life." Make the decision to educate yourself by learning the lessons your "life experiences" want to teach you! You alone can make the choice to become the receiver of truth and wisdom, or to be the uninspired student who sits in the classroom and chooses not to pay attention.

Life has taught me many lessons, and for some of them I have paid a very high price. It is commonly said, "We live and we learn," yet that's not always the case. Too many times I have chosen to learn things the hard way and missed the lesson. Somehow at the time, it seemed like a good idea and the best thing for me to do. I am happy to say that after many years of seeking wisdom, I have found easier and softer ways to live a best and blessed life today.

"If we could sell our experiences for what they cost us, we'd all be millionaires."
—Abigail Van Buren - "Dear Abby" Columnist (1918-2013)

As long as you are breathing, your reality is changing and expanding through the passing or not passing of your tests in life.

24

Your mental action and emotional reaction is based on how you decide to respond toward everything that is happening to you. What keeps things interesting is the simple truth that when you pass one test, you'll be given another one to take.

We are all part of an imperfect race, living in a fallen place, where troubles, problems, and difficulties are part of being in this world. We love and we hate. We succeed and we fail. We do right and we do wrong. We make good decisions and bad choices, every day of our lives.

You have come into this world of body, mind, and spirit to learn the lessons you need to create a life worth loving. Living this day and learning this day are one and the same. Within every perceived pain, pleasure, triumph, and defeat, we are given many opportunities to learn, change, grow, and prosper. Everything happens for a reason, only when you choose to receive the inspired wisdom and awareness from everything you think, do, and feel.

"Wherever we are and whatever we are doing, it is possible to learn something that can enrich our lives and the lives of others. Nobody's education is ever complete."
— Sir John Templeton - Philanthropist (1912-2008)

During your problems and afflictions, triumphs and solutions, you will be receiving some of your finest education...

There is no joy without some pain, no sunshine without the rain. No freedom without some limitations, no laughter without some tears. No good without some bad, no prosperity without some losses. No courage without some fear, no success without some failures. No health without sickness, no life without death. No happiness without some sadness, no love without some hate. No light without the darkness, no finish without the start.

Pain and pleasure are both great teachers. When you choose to use it all for good, healing and change are the fruits you'll pick from your tree of life. It is not a perfect process, and it isn't always an enjoyable journey. The secret to your success is to focus more on the solutions than your problems.

> "Your living is determined not so much by what life brings to you, as by the attitude you bring to life. Not so much by what happens to you, as by the way your mind looks at what happens."
> — Kahlil Gibran – Author of *The Prophet* (1883-1931)

Every day I become more aware that I have a choice in how I respond to everything that happens to me. Ninety-nine percent of your life experience is about how you react to the 100 percent of what is happening to you. The excellent or awful thing you have gone through opens up the inspired opportunities for achieving better thinking, exciting change, and increased awareness.

We are all spiritual beings, having a physical experience called "Life." When you were born, you weren't given a spirit of fear but a spirit of faith, love, power, and a positive mind. We are connected to all things, and our energy touches everything in a positive or negative way.

"Knowing yourself is the beginning of all wisdom."
— Aristotle - Tutor of Alexander The Great (384BC-322BC)

We are all a divine work in progress. There are no perfect people, places, or things. We all will encounter many losses and victories as we go through the inspirational highs and educating lows on our journey along the path of life. Nothing in this world stays the same. Everything and everyone is constantly changing.

You are a developing work of art, taking form with every brush stroke of living breath, as you cast your paint upon the canvas of life. Your life is filled with a rainbow of colors, which inspire your thoughts, feelings, choices, and actions. You can choose dark or bright shades, happy or sad tones, or pigments that are uplifting or depressing. This is the "Art of Living." So take a moment, step back from the easel, and ask yourself, "What colors am I painting my life's masterpiece with?"

The whole spectrum of human emotions is what makes this human experience so rich. There is no such thing as a good or bad emotion. They are simply emotions we are equipped with, so we can experience life to its fullest. I believe that through the learning of our lessons, we can gradually master and rise above these emotions, so we can live a better life today.

You are writing your own life story. Every thought is a word. Every feeling is a sentence. Every action forms a paragraph that defines who you are. Each day is a chapter within every created page of your life. Your heart, mind, and soul is the book. What pages are you writing? What stories are you telling?

You are the author of your own best seller, written with the ink of your free-will choices. What you decide to fill your book with is up to you! You can produce your life's work as a romance novel, a horror story, or an inspirational book. What matters most is what you have written in your heart. Whether it has a happy or sad ending is left for you to decide. Every morning, you get another chance to begin again by learning from your past and being grateful for the new opportunities your life is setting before you.

THE FUTURE IS UNWRITTEN... you are the author, sculptor, and painter, the pen, the chisel, and the brush. There are pages to write, sculptures to cast, and pictures to paint. You are the director and composer of your life. You create your own universe and live in your own world. The atmosphere is your thinking, the environment is your feelings, and the creator is your actions and reactions. As a person thinks, feels, and does, so his or her world is painted, sculpted, and written.

"Cease to be a disobedient child in the school of experience, and begin to learn with humility and patience the lessons that are set for your ultimate perfection."
— James Allen - Author of *As a Man Thinketh* (1864-1912)

All the thinking that has made my choices, every feeling that has inspired my actions, has created the life I am living right now. Once you have embraced this expanded awareness, there are no longer any perceived failures, meaningless problems, or useless mistakes in life. There is only your perception of the outcome as being the way, or not being the way, you wanted things to turn out. We all have a higher calling to live the life we were born to live. Don't let the "I can'ts" together with the "If I onlys" rob you of the life you were born to be living.

When you get different results than what you originally planned, you are given the opportunity to learn from your experience and to accomplish the changes you need to make. How you think and feel things could, would, and should have been determines whether you have a positive or negative experience based on how things really are. Good or bad, happy or sad, your life unfolds according to the way you choose to see it.

> "The best journeys in life answer questions, that in the beginning you didn't even think to ask. When everything goes wrong or not according to your plans, that's when the real adventure begins."
> — Jeff Johnson - Writer, Surf Photographer

· · · · · · ·

"Life School" began for me when I was ten years old. It was a day like any other day. I woke up, had breakfast, and got ready for the fourth grade. My mom made my peanut butter and jelly sandwhich and put it in my lunchbox, while my dog Sam barked at me to take him for his morning walk.

I remember telling my dad how excited I was that he'd be coming to my little league baseball game when he got home from work. I had gotten so much better since my opening game, when he watched me nervously step up to the plate, swing, and strike out! I looked forward to showing him how his practicing with me had helped me become a better baseball player. He grabbed his briefcase, kissed his wife and six kids goodbye, and went off to work.

At around four o'clock the same day, I watched my mother answer the phone and begin to cry hysterically. With a look of pain and disbelief on her face, she said, "Daddy got in an accident. I have to go to the hospital. Please go outside and play with your friends."

When my mom got home, she took us all into the family room, and nervously prepared to tell us something. With life-changing grief pouring from her face, she said, "Daddy won't be coming home anymore."

My father fell from a twelve-story parking garage building while walking to his car to return home to be with his family. No one will ever know, for sure, why and how it happened. It was a tragic accident, a life-changing mistake, which cost me and my dad the life we were meant to have together.

I never got to say goodbye or show him my winning swing. As tears fell from my eyes, I began the childlike process of absorbing the impact of his fall. Later, as I stared into the bathroom mirror already fogged with my tears of pain, I cried out to God... "How could You have allowed this to happen to my dad? Why? Why! Why?" While crying myself to sleep that night, I hoped and prayed that when I woke up, it all would have been a dream.

> "There is a sacredness in tears. They are not the mark of weakness, but of power. They speak more eloquently than ten thousand tongues. They are messengers of overwhelming grief and unspeakable love."
> — Washington Irving - Author of *The Legend of Sleepy Hollow* (1783-1859)

Over fifty years have gone by since that life-changing day. Growing up without a father was not my choice, but how I handled it was! At a young and innocent age, I learned that unexpected pain and losses are a part of this great adventure called "My Life."

· · · · · · ·

There are some things in life we can control, and many other situations we can't. Life never turns out exactly how we imagined it would. That is when love, gratitude, forgiveness and a positive mental attitude make all the difference in your world. Life is not an event; it's a day-to-day process.

> "Every choice you make has an end result. You cannot tailor-make the situations in life, but you can tailor-make the attitudes to fit those situations. Positive thinking will let you do everything better than negative thinking will."
> — Zig Ziglar - Author of *Born To Win* (1926–2012)

One of the biggest mistakes we can make in life is to think we shouldn't have any problems. We think difficulties are a curse when they can actually be a blessing and a gift. They have the potential to stimulate us into using our heart, mind, and soul for gaining more understanding of our "Higher Self." Our greatest growth often takes place when we are faced with a problem that forces us to change and progress into becoming a better, wiser person.

Just think about how much it costs to go through four years of college. We pay many thousands of dollars to learn a skill, a profession, and to get a degree. We spend billions of tax dollars each year teaching students history, math, English, and science. Granted, these are very important subjects. Yet traditional education doesn't teach us how to manage our personal finances in math class. Or how to create an effective job resume in economics or English class. Or how to find happiness, know love, ask for forgiveness, deal with problems, and live a satisfying life in health class.

We are taught in school how to add, subtract, multiply, and divide, yet we were never taught how to measure our own self-worth or what is truly valuable in life. An educational system isn't worth a great deal if it teaches people how to make a living, but it doesn't teach them how to make a meaningful life filled with happiness, health, peace, and love.

The Nobel Prize winning physicist, whose name, Albert Einstein, is synonymous with the word genius, said it like this… "The only source of knowledge is experience. Education is what remains, after one has forgotten what one has learned in school."

I grew up in a small New Jersey town called Point Pleasant Beach. My entire senior graduating high school class of 1972 had a little over one hundred classmates. I was an above average student, and I had a sense that I had a bright future ahead of me. I truly felt I had received a good education, yet I always had a sense that much of what I had been taught would have little to do with what I would need to be successful in the real world.

I knew I wasn't going to college to study to be a doctor, lawyer, or an accountant. I believed I was going to be a salesman like my father was, and the education I needed wasn't available in the traditional educational system. During my first year of college, I realized I was just repeating what I had already learned in high school.

On the semester break, I came home from Ocean County College and told my mom that I was going to "Life School." She didn't have a clue what I was talking about! I explained to her that I needed to travel and encounter the real world while gaining knowledge and wisdom through my learning experiences. That I wanted to learn the things that weren't taught in the classroom and I needed to enroll in the courses of "Living Life." I felt my time and money would be better spent on getting a "Real Life Education" from the "University of Life."

"Don't let your schooling, interfere with your education."
— Mark Twain - Author of *The Adventures of Huckleberry Finn* (1835-1910)

I packed my suitcase, snorkel gear, and surfboard, bought the plane tickets, and tuned up the camper van. With two of my good friends, I hit the road of "Inspirational Knowledge" and headed for Florida, the Bahamas, Puerto Rico, the Virgin Islands, Mexico, California and Hawaii.

• • • • • • •

Peter, Dicky, and I came to the island of Eleuthera in the Bahamas, to dive, surf, and seek adventure. We were sharing our rented home with two guys who had come to the island to do some big game fishing. They weren't having much luck catching fish and there wasn't any surf, so we came up with the great idea to go and watch the sharks being fed. Entertainment wasn't easy to find on this small Caribbean Island, and seeing this rare event would offer us an exciting and educational experience.

Around noon the next day, we stuffed the five of us into our fisherman friend's rented Volkswagen Bug and drove down the coral paved road that would take us to the Hatchet Bay Chicken Factory.

Twice a day, the poultry processing plant loaded the bloody chicken parts and dead bodies into a dump truck and cast them into the sea. The Bahamas were formed from limestone and coral, so the truck could dump them in a place where you could drive across an ancient rock reef, right up to a fifty foot deep drop off that plunged from the island's edge.

With a swarm of flies buzzing around the smelly truck, the driver backed it up to the ocean's edge, while ten to fifteen foot sharks waited to be served their favorite meal. As the rotting

34

meat poured into the warm blue water, the sharks lifted their enormous heads to bite into a delicious whole chicken or to swallow a mouthful of poultry parts. These colossal predators were being spoon-fed daily by the truck load and they were growing into gigantic hammerhead, tiger, and bull sharks.

From Monday to Friday, when the chicken processing plant was open, these monster sharks were so well fed that we didn't worry about shark attacks while we were surfing the waves at Surfer's Beach. Yet on the weekend, it wasn't uncommon to spot a shark, as the waves broke across the crystal clear reef. On Saturdays and Sundays, these large sharks cruised down the beach looking for a meal that tasted like chicken!

Shark hunting was becoming very popular in the islands, and while we were watching the Hatchet Bay feeding frenzy, our fisherman friends saw an opportunity for us to catch the Big One!

The key to catching a giant shark is to have a powerful reel, a large hook, and strong fishing line. Yet there seemed to be one challenging problem! Our friends' fishing gear was great for catching big fish, but not strong enough to be messing around with these enormous carnivores of the sea. We were hungry for adventure and knew we would figure out a way to carry out our wild and crazy plan.

"You don't always need a plan. Sometimes you just need to breathe, trust, let go and see what happens."
— Mandy Hale - Author of *The Single Woman*

After a few days of brain-storming, my thoughts were interrupted by the sound of our friend's Volkswagen Bug. I suddenly realized that we had the ultimate shark fishing gear right before our eyes. We could use the Volkswagen Bug as the reel, 100 feet or so of steel chain as our fishing line, a grappling hook, a floatation buoy, and a few dead chickens to catch one of these mighty beasts of prey!

Our idea was to hook into a shark, and then pull it out of the water onto the dry reef. With the human power of five strong, wild, and crazy guys, combined with the horsepower of the Volkswagen Bug, we believed we would be strong enough to overpower the shark.

What were we thinking? What were we going to do once we caught a massive shark? What would happen when the wildly flopping body and gnashing teeth were out of the water and onto the reef? We weren't really sure what we were going to do, but we were ready! I had a baseball bat, my spear gun, and a few big rocks for protection, just in case things went wrong!

When we arrived at the Hatchet Bay shark feeding location, I crawled under the car and attached the u-bolt and chain to the vehicle's metal frame. The huge sharks came within a few feet of the reef's edge as we watched them bite into their floating lunch. The idea of carrying out what we were planning kept us in nervous anticipation and excited fear.

I threw the hook, line, and chickens as far as I could cast them. As the floatation buoy brought the bait within striking distance, the hungry sharks were everywhere. There were schools of them, gorging themselves in a bloody, feeding frenzy. Their enormous teeth glistened in the hot Bahama sun as they chewed and swallowed their feast of sun-baked chicken parts. None of us had ever done anything like this before and it was now a sport fishing reality. The line was tossed, the bait was cast, and it was too late to chicken out!

> "If you want to improve yourself, be content to
> be thought of as foolish and stupid."
> — Epictetus - Greek Philosopher (55AD-135AD)

A giant fin was circling the bait. The shark seemed to sense that something wasn't quite right. We weren't sure whether it would seize our luscious lure, or take one of the floating chickens that had no strings attached.

It bumped the buoy, made a few dives under the water and then struck the lifeless flesh with the awesome power of an ancient predator. Before we could react, the steel chain was reeling off the reef with a metallic zipping sound. The wheels of the Volkswagen Bug spun backwards out of control. The fight was on between man and beast and we were pushing the car with all the strength we had.

The magnificent creature was going crazy! The shark jumped high into the air and viciously shook its head in an attempt to get loose from the hook. It was thrashing and fighting as if we had a Blue Marlin on the line. As the smoking tires skidded across the jagged reef, we got closer and closer to the ocean's edge.

Our panicked driver began to open the car door as he realized we were losing this tug of war! His job was to reel in this enormous fish, but in his fear, he decided it was time to bail out and save his own skin. He set the brake and jumped out of the car. Always remember that when things go wrong, try your hardest not to go with them.

As the gigantic shark pulled the Volkswagen Bug into the ocean, the car rolled over and began to sink. The shark struggled desperately to get loose from the vehicle it was chained to. Then suddenly, with one last enormous jump and powerful shake of its head, the shark spit out the hook and set itself free!

We had arrived seeking adventure, but instead, our biggest fear had come true. We had lost the car and the Big One got away, it was now sunken treasure at the bottom of the sea!

Nothing had worked out the way we planned it. We were exhausted and couldn't believe what had just happened. I looked around and was so thankful that no one got hurt, not even the shark!

"Only those who dare to fail greatly, can ever achieve greatly."
— Robert Kennedy – 64th U. S. Attorney General (1925-1968)

It was a long and hungry walk home, with no car or shark steaks for dinner. We knew nobody would believe our fish story about

"The Big One that got away," so we all agreed to keep the story to ourselves. People did wonder where the Volkswagen Bug was! Had the rental car been returned, stolen, or lost at sea?

"Live life fully while you're here. Experience everything. Have fun, be crazy, be weird. Go out and screw up! You're going to anyway, so you might as well enjoy the process. Take the opportunity to learn from your mistakes."
— Anthony Robbins – Author of *Awaken The Giant Within*

You may be asking yourself, what could Rob possibly have learned from this experience? Looking back many years, I learned that some of my best ideas and good intentions sometimes didn't work out the way I wanted them to. I learned that through my weaknesses, I am made strong. I learned to make every experience educational, my life meaningful, and my wrong choices inspirational. I also realized that through my failures and successes, I'm given the opportunity to learn some of my greatest lessons. Oh… and not to mess around with big and powerful sharks!

· · · · · · ·

ADVICE FOR BETTER LIVING…

★ Great love and great accomplishments require risk and taking chances.

★ Not getting what you wanted is sometimes a stroke of luck and the answer to your prayers, desires and wishes.

* When you make a mistake, admit it, correct it, learn from it, and become a wiser and better person because of it.

* Let go of your excuses and always take responsibility for your actions.

* When you lose, become a winner by not losing the lesson.

* What you make of your life is up to you. No one can give you the life you want to be living.

* You can't change the past, only the present. What has already happened can either inspire you or destroy you!

* No matter how many self-help books you read or lessons you have learned, what good will they do if you don't act upon them?

• • • • • • •

"While life may not always be fair, you must never allow the pains, hurdles, and handicaps of the moment to poison your attitude. You can never win when you wear the ugly cloak of self-pity and the sour sound of whining will certainly frighten away any opportunity for success."
— Og Mandino - Author of *A Better Way to Live* (1923-1996)

Believing you have a purpose, plan, and destiny for your life gives meaning to everything you are experiencing. When the student is ready, the teacher will appear. When the mind is ready, confusion will disappear. When the heart is ready, love will fill the air. When faith is flowing, it will wash away all fear.

Choosing to learn from your experiences and to stop dwelling over your already lived past focuses you on the hope of the future. The only place we can live is in the "Now" which in a moment becomes your "Past" and in a second turns your "Future" into your "Present." It's all about what you learn from it, what you do with it, and how you use it.

One lesson at a time, we gain the power to change and learn from our mistakes and bad decisions. We can use the wrong direction as a compass to point us in the right direction. We can turn our bad choices into better decisions, failures into successes, breakdowns into startups, destruction into construction, losses into gains, and a poor performance into an Oscar.

"Everyone gets the experience, only some get the lesson."
—T. S. Eliot – Nobel Prize Winner, Author of *Dante* (1888-1965)

• • • • • • •

It was 1973 and we had driven from New Jersey to Florida, flown to the Bahamas and Puerto Rico, and then we drove from Florida, 3000 miles deep down into the heart of Mexico.

We were camping in a beachfront coconut grove on the Pacific Coast shoreline. Under the light of the full moon, you could see the shadows of the waving palm leaves and hear the sounds of the creaking coconut trees. It was a hot and sticky tropical evening and the Volkswagen Van wasn't a comfortable place for four sweating guys to be sleeping together!

We had been in the area for over a month, surfing a break on Petacalco Bay known as "The Mexican Pipeline." We were planning on driving back up north as soon as our money-gram arrived at the local Western Union office. We had already spent months living in the beach town of San Blas, surfing the longest wave in the world on Matanchen Bay, and we were all looking forward to going back.

We had already been warned that anything could happen this deep down into Mexico and some of us slept with knifes at our side. We had to bribe our way across the United States/Mexican border at Nogales, Arizona, because surfer guys like us with long hair were not allowed a visa to travel into the country. There weren't many Americans around, and if anything happened, no one would know about it!

We were young and fearless, and we felt that the most dangerous thing we would encounter were the many sharks and the power of these killer waves! As "Gringos" in a foreign country, Mexico seemed to be quite lawless. It wasn't uncommon to get harassed by the local police, known as the "Federales," who were still wearing a belt of bullets across their chests and carrying loaded machine guns.

You see, the reason we were all sleeping in the van was because there were too many mosquitoes to sleep under the stars. The camper van had screens on the windows, a pop-up top, and would provide us with an element of security. In the middle of the night, Dicky decided to string his hammock between two coconut trees and brave the mosquitoes, instead of dealing with the snoring and too close for comfort conditions!

It was about three in the morning when the van door opened and woke us into a startled defensive mode! Peter grabbed his buck knife and I grabbed a flashlight. A very drunk and angry man had a machete against Dicky's throat, while he was slurring his demands for money. He wanted 5000 pesos, which was about $400 in American money. He said if we didn't give him the money he wanted, he would cut Dicky's throat!

We weren't thrilled about the idea of him robbing us of the money we hadn't even gotten yet! The truth of the matter was that if he succeeded, we would have to go back to New Jersey in the middle of the winter, and that wasn't going to happen! Jersey was ice cold, full wetsuit weather, and we were surfing perfect uncrowded warm water waves, in an endless summer of tropical sun.

I told Peter to put his knife away and to let me handle it! I had spent two years in high school Spanish class and I was now under pressure to do some hostage negotiating. I started by telling the robber that we were rich Americans sleeping in our car because someone else had already robbed us of all our money. We were here, instead of in a hotel, because we were waiting for the Western Union money to be wired to us. I told him I would gladly give him the money he demanded from us today, when we got our cash tomorrow. He said he was willing to accept my offer, if we would put it in writing. I explained that we would show our good faith, by giving him an IOU for the money he hadn't stolen from us yet!

"In any moment of decision, the best thing you can do is the right thing, the next best thing is the wrong thing, and the worst thing you can do is nothing. After all, if you do the wrong thing, at least you can learn."
— Theodore Roosevelt – 26th U.S. President (1858-1919)

I nervously searched for a blank piece of paper, wrote out the details of our agreement, signed my name, and asked everyone to put their signature on the promissory note for the money the robber would steal from us tomorrow. I gasped a sigh of relief as the assailant removed the knife from Dicky's bleeding throat. When the document was passed back to me, I looked at their names which read, Peter Pan and Dick Tracy. The drunken thief said, "Muchas Gracias" and grabbed his IOU. He said he would be back at high noon tomorrow to collect his not yet stolen cash!

We slept a few hours until sunrise and then fled the scene of the crime as fast as we could. We laughed about the fact that our "Would-Be Robber" had only a hangover and a worthless piece of paper, instead of our money! We were all still alive and had a life-changing story to share with our friends and family when we got home safely.

"Life is a series of experiences, each one of which makes us bigger, even though it is hard to realize this. For the world was

built to develop character, and we must learn that the setbacks and griefs which we endure, help us in our marching onward."
— Henry Ford - Automobile Industrialist (1863-1947)

So what do you think I learned from this experience? Patience? Trusting my instincts? The power of persuasion? Boldness, self-confidence, controlling my emotions and getting in touch with my fears? Especially when someone else's life depended on the grades I got in Spanish class!

. . . .

"Remember that there is growth and learning in every experience and encounter, whether you choose to label it good or bad. Get in the habit of looking for it, finding it and applying it."
— Kim Somers Egelsee - Author of *Getting Your Life to a Ten Plus*

COURSE TWO

Celebrating Your Life

There is no one else like you on this planet. You are a one-of-a kind creation, and there will never be another person just like you. You are a special and unique individual, a priceless miracle of love and divine design. What do you have if you don't love yourself? What do you possess if you gain the whole world and lose your own soul? You are enrolled in the "You University," and you alone can take and grade your own tests. Decide to become who you want to be, right from where you are. Wake up and celebrate the love and grace of a new day of being yourself.

"Today you are you, that is truer than true.
There is no one alive, who is You-er than you."
— Dr. Seuss - Author of *Happy Birthday to You* (1904-1991)

YOU ARE A GIFT TO THE WORLD... your presence is priceless to everyone around you. So don't let anything or anyone steal your self-worth way. Recognize and acknowledge your own incredible value by accepting who you are and allowing yourself to be "good enough". If you choose to put a low value on yourself, the world won't raise your price-less-ness. Use your self-awareness to increase your self-worth, by acknowledging the value of the present... your self-esteem is wrapped up in!

47

"You are beautifully enough! Your stories of "not good enough" are fictional novels, written by a culture still hiding its light under a bushel of shame. The real story, your true autobiography, is one of inherent magnificence, courage and divinity flowing through your soul-veins. So you decide which book to read... the fictional novel written by those who do not see you, or the holy book written by your glorious spirit."
— Jeff Brown - Author of *Ascending With Both Feet On The Ground*

We are always in the process of learning to love ourselves more and more each day. Even when we are not liking ourselves, we are still in the "Love Learning Process." When the party is over and everyone goes home, you will always be left with yourself.

"The spiritual journey is not about acquiring something outside yourself, rather, you are penetrating deep layers and veils to return to the deepest truth of your own being."
— Ram Dass - Author of *Be Here Now*

Michael Beckwith, well-known New Thought minister in the movie *The Secret*, teaches… "I believe that you are great, that there is something magnificent about you. This power within you that's greater than the world, it will begin to emerge. It will take over your life. It will feed you, clothe you, guide you, protect you, direct you, sustain your very existence, if you let it!"

You are the new gold being made upon this earth, the new diamonds formed by pressure and dirt. You are a precious and priceless gem, yet only you can calculate your own self-worth.

· · · · · · ·

ARE YOU WORTH MORE THAN $20?

A well-known speaker started off his seminar by holding up a $20 bill. In the room of two hundred, he asked, "Who would like this $20 bill?"

Hands started going up. He said, "I am going to give this $20 to one of you, but first let me do this." He proceeded to crumple the dollar bill up. He then asked, "Who still wants it?" Still the hands were up in the air.

"Well," he replied, "what if I do this?" And he dropped it on the ground and started to grind it into the floor with his shoe. He picked it up, now crumpled and dirty. "Now who still wants it?" Still the hands went into the air.

Finally, he said, "My friends, you have all learned a very valuable lesson. No matter what I did to the money, you still wanted it, because it did not decrease in value. It was still worth $20."

Many times in our lives, we are dropped, crumpled, and ground into the dirt by the decisions we make and the circumstances that come our way. We feel as though we are worthless. But no matter what has happened or what will happen, you will never lose your value.

While the value of a $20 bill could never be increased, our value as human beings can, if instead of despairing from our setbacks and failures, we turn them into lessons that enrich our experience, that serve as stepping stones on our path of life.

Wisdom comes mostly from experience, and experience comes only from decisions, good ones and bad ones. Just like how a good sailor is made by the rough seas, our value becomes more valuable, from bouncing back from setbacks and emerging from difficulties.

So, whenever you feel broken, crumpled, or ground into the dirt, remember the $20 bill, and remember that you are an appreciating asset if you learn to appreciate that every adversity is a learning opportunity and then learn from it.

· · · · · · ·

BE YOURSELF, AND LOVE YOURSELF... You can only love others, to the same degree that you love, honor, and respect yourself. It is simply a matter of emotional math. You can't give to someone something you don't already have. You can't withdraw money from an empty bank account. You need gas in the tank to take a trip. When you run away from your light, you'll always cast a shadow on the world around you. Always love yourself unconditionally, while forgiving yourself persistently, no matter what the circumstances are! Love yourself for who you were yesterday, who you are today, and who you will be tomorrow.

> "To be yourself in a world that is constantly trying to make you something else, is the greatest accomplishment."
> — Ralph Waldo Emerson - Essayist, "Nature" (1803-1882)

I CAN ONLY BE ME... Compared to you, I am no one! Within myself, I am everyone. Compared to what you have, I have nothing! Within myself, I have everything.

"The biggest message is for you to just be who you are. That's why you've come here, to express your magnificence and to shine your light as brightly as you can. Don't deprive the universe or the world of who you came here to be."

—Anita Moorjani - Author of *Dying To Be Me*

We waste too much of our precious time comparing other peoples' outside to whom we are on our inside and then we lose a part of ourselves in the process! Choose to be a first class version of yourself, instead of a second class version of somebody you think you should be like. There is no such thing as living in someone else's shoes or seeing life through someone else's eyes. The only shoes you can wear are on your own two feet, and the only eyes you can see with are your own. If you can't be yourself, then who can you be? It would be like the river's foolish dreams to be the sea!

"What lies behind us and what lies ahead of us, are tiny matters compared to what lies within us."

— Henry S. Haskins - Author of *Meditations in Wall Street* (1875-1957)

WE ARE ALL CONNECTED... with every heartbeat and breath. The thirteenth century poet, Rumi, writes, "You are not just a drop in the ocean, you are the mighty ocean in the drop." Mother Teresa, the icon of charity, writes, "We sometimes feel what we're doing and who we are is just a drop in the ocean. Yet the ocean would be much less, because of that missing drop which is you."

· · · · · · ·

REBELLION AGAINST THE STOMACH

Once a man had a dream in which his hands, feet, mouth, and brain all began to rebel against his stomach. "You good-for-nothing sluggard!" the hands said, "We work all day long sawing, hammering, lifting, and carrying. By evening, we're covered with blisters and scratches, our joints ache, and we're covered with dirt. Meanwhile, you just sit there hogging the food."

"We agree!" cried the feet. "Think how sore we get, walking back and forth all day long. And you just stuff yourself full, so that you're that much heavier to carry around."

"That's right!" whined the mouth. "Where do you think all that food you love comes from? I'm the one who has to chew it all up, and as soon as I'm finished, you suck it all down for yourself. Do you call that fair?"

"And what about me?" said the brain. "Do you think it's easy being up here, having to think about where your next meal is going to come from? And yet I get nothing at all for my pains."

And one by one the parts of the body joined the complaint against the stomach, which didn't say anything at all. "I have an idea," the brain announced. "Let's all rebel against the lazy belly and stop working for it."

"Superb idea!" all the other members and organs agreed. "We'll teach you how important we are, you glutton. Then maybe you'll do a little work of your own."

So they all stopped working. The hands refused to do lifting and carrying. The feet refused to walk. The mouth promised not to chew or swallow a single bite. And the brain swore it wouldn't come up with any more bright ideas.

At first, the stomach growled a bit, as it always did when it was hungry. But after a while, it was quiet. Then, to the dreaming man's surprise, he found he could not walk. He could not grasp anything in his hands. He could not even open his mouth. And suddenly, he began to feel very ill.

The dream seemed to go on for several days. As each day passed, the man felt worse and worse. "The rebellion had better not last much longer," he thought to himself, "or I will starve!"

Meanwhile, the hands, feet, mouth, and brain just lay there getting weaker and weaker. At first they roused themselves just enough to taunt the stomach every once in awhile. But before long, they didn't even have the energy to do that!

Finally, the man heard a faint voice coming from the direction of his feet. "It could be that we were all wrong," they were saying. "We suppose the stomach might have been working in his own way all along!" "I was just thinking the same thing," murmured the brain. "It's true that he's been getting all the food, but it seems he's been sending most of it right back to us."

"We might as well admit we were wrong," the mouth said. "The stomach has just as much work to do as the hands, feet, brain, and teeth." "Then let's get back to work," they all cried together. And with that the man woke up from his dream.

To his relief, he discovered his feet could walk, his hands could grasp, his mouth could chew, and his brain could now think clearly. He began to feel so much better. "Well, there is a lesson in this dream for me," he thought as he filled his stomach with breakfast. "Either we all work together or nothing works at all."

· · · · · · ·

"One of the most beautiful compensations of this life, is that no man can sincerely try to help another, without helping himself."
— Ralph Waldo Emerson - Poet, "The Snow Storm" (1803-1882)

It's not about how much stuff you have, or how popular you are. It's all about how you feel about yourself at the end of the day, and how comfortable you are living in your own skin. You will be important to some and insignificant to others. You can hide everything from other people, yet you can never hide anything from your authentic self. Be the best you can be by being fully present in your self-becoming moments. Whatever happens in life, your best friend should always be you.

"You are more than the shoes on your feet, the designer dress on your back, the purse you carry, or the money inside of your wallet. You and I are more than the stuff, more than the things in our lives. Somewhere between our things and our stuff is us."
— *Bobby* movie 2006

I send this "Happy Birthday Message" to my Facebook friends on their day of celebration… "Life should not be measured by the number of years you have lived, but by the love shared, the memories made, the joy given, and the blessings received. Live for today and love your tomorrows. Laugh at all of your yesterdays and never regret your past. Always hope for the future and cherish every moment you still have. Life is not measured by the number of breaths you take, but by the moments that take your breath away."

No matter what you need to do in your life, you'll need help doing it! There is absolutely nothing you'll ever do that will be done totally by yourself. There is always someone, or something, either directly or indirectly, influencing, inspiring, or helping you accomplish your goals, dreams and desires.

"As you grow older you will discover that you have two hands. One for helping yourself and the other for helping others."
— Audrey Hepburn - Actress, Humanitarian (1929-1993)

· · · · · · ·

THE MOUSE TRAP

A mouse looked through the crack in the wall to see the farmer and his wife open a package. "What food might this contain?" the mouse wondered. He was devastated to discover it was a mousetrap.

Retreating to the farmyard, the mouse proclaimed the warning, "There is a mousetrap in the house! There is a mousetrap in the house!" The chicken clucked and scratched, raised her head, and said, "Mr. Mouse, I can tell this is a grave concern to you, but it is of no consequence to me. I cannot be bothered by it."

The mouse turned to the pig and told him, "There is a mouse-trap in the house! There is a mousetrap in the house!" The pig sympathized, but said, "I am so very sorry, Mr. Mouse, but there is nothing I can do about it but pray. Be assured you are in my prayers."

The mouse turned to the cow and said, "There is a mousetrap in the house! There is a mousetrap in the house!" The cow said, "Wow, Mr. Mouse. I'm sorry for you, but it's no skin off my nose."

So, the mouse returned to the house, head down and dejected, to face the farmer's mousetrap alone. That very night, a sound was heard throughout the house, like the sound of a mouse-trap catching its prey. The farmer's wife rushed to see what was caught. In the darkness, she did not see it was a venomous snake whose tail the trap had caught. The snake bit the farmer's wife.

The farmer rushed her to the hospital and she returned home with a fever. Everyone knows you treat a fever with fresh chicken soup. So the farmer took his hatchet to the farmyard for the soup's main ingredient. But his wife's sickness continued, so friends and neighbors came to sit with her around the clock. To feed them, the farmer butchered the pig.

The farmer's wife did not get well. So many people came for her funeral that the farmer had the cow slaughtered to provide enough meat for all of them. The mouse looked upon it all, from his crack in the wall, with great sadness.

So, the next time you hear someone is facing a problem and think it doesn't concern you, remember that when one of us is threatened, we are all at risk. We are all involved in this journey called life. We must keep an eye out for one another and make an extra effort to encourage one another. Each of us is a vital thread in another person's tapestry.

• • • • • • •

"We cannot live only for ourselves. A thousand fibers connect us with our fellow men and among those fibers, as sympathetic threads, our actions run as causes, and they come back to us as effects."

— Herman Melville – Author of *Moby Dick* (1819-1891)

• • • • • • •

LIVE TODAY... like it's your last day on earth and you know exactly how you want to be living your life.

WORK TODAY… like you love your job, you don't need any more money, and your career is to enjoy life.

LAUGH TODAY… like small children do, seeing the humor in life and having the ability to laugh at yourself.

GIVE TODAY… without expecting anything in return, knowing you will always receive when you give with a thankful heart.

DANCE TODAY… without a care in the world, expressing your love for life and the joy of living.

TRUST TODAY... as if you had nothing to lose and everything to gain.

LOVE TODAY... like your heart has never been broken and you deserve to give and have all the love in the world.

LEARN TODAY... for knowledge, wisdom, and experience are the keys for opening up the doors, into living your best life today.

. . . .

"The more you praise and celebrate your life,
the more there is in life to celebrate."
— Oprah Winfrey - From her *"Life Class"* on OWN TV

COURSE THREE

What Are You Thinking?

Thinking is the soul talking to itself.

Thoughts are things, very powerful things. What you're experiencing is the direct result of what you are choosing to think about. You can't think a negative and a positive thought at the same time! Therefore it's your last thought and feeling that has created your happiness or pain, joy or suffering. For as a person thinks in his or her heart, so he or she is.

Your best thinking has gotten you to where you are today. The life you are living right now is the result of every thought and feeling you've ever had. For better or for worse, for richer or for poorer, in sickness and in health, your thoughts have created who you are at this very moment. So ask yourself this question, "Who and what, am I thinking myself into being today?"

"Education is not the learning of facts, but the training of the mind to think. The significant problems we face, can't be solved by the same level of thinking that created them."
—Albert Einstein - Genius Physicist (1879-1955)

TAKE CONTROL OF YOUR THOUGHTS... for it is your thoughts alone that cause you pain or pleasure. Nothing outside of your mind can affect you, without your consent. Thoughts are like branches extending from a thinking tree. They will either bear sweet and healthy fruit, or produce food for thought which is sour and spoiled. What kind of fruit is your tree producing?

Take this moment to close your eyes and visualize yourself with everything you've always wanted and doing what you have always dreamed about doing. The universe is full of abundance, and you are either rich in thought or poor in impoverished thinking. Don't miss the moment where you are whole, loved, healthy, and fulfilled... right now! When you change the way you think and feel about your life, your inner and outer worlds change and you begin to live your best life today.

"Our self-image and our habits tend to go together. Change one and you will automatically change the other."
— Dr. Maxwell Maltz - Author of *Psycho-Cybernetics* (1889-1975)

YOU NEED TO THINK MORE ABOUT, WHAT YOU'RE THINKING ABOUT... You can think yourself into a good or bad mood, a great or a lousy day, and an okay or exceptional life. You are the only person in control or out of control of your thoughts, feelings, and actions. Your life will become much better when you decide to begin thinking that your life is better! Think good thoughts, for you'll never rise any higher than your mind allows you to go.

THE BATTLE WITHIN THE MIND... Everyone experiences a mental conflict, where good and bad thoughts are at war with each other. It is on this battlefield where we either experience victory or defeat!

WHAT ARE YOU THINKING

"The happiness of your life depends upon the
quality of your thoughts."
— Marcus Aurelius - Roman Emperor (121AD-180AD)

HOW DO YOU THINK MORE POSITIVELY?... When you choose to become aware of what you are thinking about, the first thing you will be amazed by is the number of negative thoughts you actually have in a single day. When you have a negative thought, you must first become mindful of it, then capture it, and replace it with a positive one. When you choose to be thinking your best possible thoughts, you begin to win the battle. It's a daily struggle which is won within the heart, mind, and soul.

"No thought lives in your head rent-free. Each thought you
have will either be an investment or a cost. It will either move
you toward happiness and success or away from it. It will
either empower you or disempower you. That's why it is
imperative, that you choose your thoughts wisely."
— T. Harv Eker - Author of *Secrets of the Millionaire Mind*

We get our daily bread, from what we bake in our heads. Our thoughts create both the feasts and the famines in our life. What kind of food are you feeding your mind? You are only as healthy as the quality of the last thought you fed to yourself. Garbage in… garbage out! I created every problem I've ever had by thinking that I had a problem. Your mind can either be your worst enemy or your best friend.

"Our subconscious minds have no sense of humor, play no jokes and cannot tell the difference between reality and an imagined thought or image. What we continually think about eventually will manifest in our lives."

— Sidney Madwed - Author of *Original Poems and Insights*

Life isn't about the things we have or what we're doing that really makes us happy or unhappy. Other people, circumstances, and things don't cause our problems. It's always a direct result of how we think and feel things are. If we fully awaken to the reality of how powerful our thoughts really are and how they create everything in our lives, we would do everything within our power never to have another negative thought! Choose your thoughts wisely. Focus on good thoughts and you will have a good life.

"If we understood the power of our thoughts, we would guard them more closely. If we understood the awesome power of our words, we would prefer silence to almost anything negative. In our thoughts and words we create our own weaknesses and strengths."

— Betty Eadie - Author of *Embraced by the Light*

· · · · · · ·

WHAT ARE YOU PLANTING INSIDE YOUR MIND?... I want to share with you an inspirational story, from Earl Nightingale's book *The Strangest Secret*, which is considered to be one of the greatest motivational writings of all time. Earl was an author, radio show host and motivational speaker, who lived from 1921 to 1989. He is known as the "Dean of Personal Development"…

Suppose a farmer has some land, and it's good, fertile land. The land gives the farmer a choice; he may plant in that land whatever he chooses. The land doesn't care. It is up to the farmer to make the decision. We're comparing the human mind with the land, because the mind, like the land, doesn't care what you plant in it. It will return what you plant, but it doesn't care what you plant.

Now, let's say that the farmer has two seeds in his hand. One is a seed of corn, the other is nightshade, a deadly poison. He digs two little holes in the earth and he plants both seeds, one corn, the other nightshade. He covers up the holes, waters and takes care of the land, and what will happen? Invariably, the land will return what was planted. As it is written in the Bible, "As ye sow, so shall ye reap."

Remember, the land doesn't care. It will return poison in just as wonderful abundance as it will corn. So up come the two plants, one corn and one poison. The human mind is far more fertile, far more incredible and mysterious than the land, but it works the same way. It doesn't care what we plant, success or failure, a concrete worthwhile goal or confusion, misunderstanding, fear, anxiety, and so on. But what we plant must return to us.

You see, the human mind is the last great unexplored continent on earth. It contains riches beyond our wildest dreams. It will return anything we want to plant. The Law of the Mind is analogous to the "Law of the Farm." The ideas that you hold in your mind reproduce after their kind. Thought seeds are just like physical seeds. So let's invest our time into thoughts, feelings, and activities, which produce the fruits of life that we want to be harvesting today.

· · · · · · ·

IT IS ALL INSIDE YOUR HEAD... Your reality is what you "Think is," "Feel is," and "Believe is." Every cell in your body listens to your thoughts and your heart creates a corresponding feeling. Every thought, good or bad, creates a bio-chemical reaction that your physical body responds to. Stress, hunger, anxiety, depression, peace, satisfaction, joy, happiness, and love are all chemical reactions in your brain, created by your thoughts. You are the only one causing your every thought and feeling and this creates our perception of how we are experiencing everything that is happening to us. All we can ever know and experience is this very moment in time, awakening to the power of being here now.

"Use your mind to change the molecular structure of circumstances. I know that it's a foreign concept to many of you, but thoughts are things and when you pour energy into formulating your thoughts and propelling them with love and amplified intent, you alter the molecular structure of circumstances, thus bringing forth a new outcome."
— Ariaa Jaeger - Author of *Ariaaisms: Spiritual Food for the Soul*

POSITIVE THINKERS... see an opportunity in every difficulty. NEGATIVE THINKERS... see the difficulty in every opportunity.

People create their reality based on what they think and feel is possible. What we think and feel creates our perspective based on the information we receive from the outside world, which we accept or reject as truth. Negative energy exists in your space because it wants to become positive energy and only you can transform it into what it wants to be. You are the instructor, teaching yourself within your own mind.

· · · · · · ·

THINKING

by Walter D. Wintle

If you think you're beaten, you are.
If you think you dare not, you won't.
If you would like to win, but you think you can't,
It's almost certain you won't.

If you think you'll lose, you've lost.
For out in the world we find.
Success begins with a person's will,
It's all in the state of mind.

If you think you're outclassed, you are.
You've got to think high to rise.
You've got to be sure of yourself before,
You can ever win a prize.

Life's battles don't always go, to the stronger or faster man.
But sooner or later, the person who wins,
Is the man or woman who thinks they can!

· · · · · · ·

Andy Andrews, author of one of my favorite books, *The Seven Decisions,* teaches that… "Circumstances do not push or pull. A person who is depressed is spending too much time thinking about the way things are now and not enough time thinking about how they want things to be."

Change the way you think, feel, and react to the things that are happening to you in everyday life and your whole world will begin to change. When we change our failure thinking into successful thinking, our negative thoughts into positive thoughts, we are guaranteed a life that's getting better, instead of more bitter every day.

So, let's say just for today, throughout your every thought and feeling, that life is great, that everyone is good, and everything is amazing. Okay? And let's say that everyone loves you, that the universe is supplying your every need and nothing is against you. All right? And if you like this game, you'll play it again tomorrow, and the next day, and pretty soon your life will become all of these things. Thoughts become realities as you transform your life by the renewing of your mind.

"It is your thinking that leads to your suffering, and your thinking can also lead to peace of mind and a sense of fulfillment."
— Charlie Badenhop - Contemporary Zen Master

. . . .

When I was in my twenties, I began to search for the higher meaning of life through books, seeking God, and going to self-help seminars. I decided to look into the very popular self-improvement course called "The EST Forum." It was the thing to do in Southern California, and everyone who took the course, was talking about how they experienced major break-throughs in their lives. It cost $500 to attend and that was more than half of the total amount of money I had in the bank. I decided to go for it and make the investment into making my life a better living experience.

The founder of EST, Werner H. Erhard, developed "The Erhard Seminar Training" as a two-weekend, sixty hour, self-awareness course. The purpose of the training was to transform one's ability to experience life on "Life's terms" and not based on the situations you are trying to change. It empowered participants to shift their minds into a state of being satisfied, and experiencing oneself as whole and complete, in the present moment. The idea of accepting all things "As is" was meant to free you from the past, and bring you into the "Now." This inspired you to let go and accept things as they are, which allowed you to get out of the way and let life take its natural course.

As I participated in the process, I experienced a very powerful, life-changing state of awakening. I was totally amazed as I watched people having major emotional break downs, while some went running out of the room hysterically crying and others passed out from sensory overload. The process was very disciplined. You couldn't speak or go to the bathroom, except when the seminar leader said you could. It was all about being a part of the process and letting go of trying to control everything in your life.

I got in touch with a lot of things I had pushed deep down inside my psyche. I relived the emotional pain of breaking up with my first love, putting my childhood dog Sam to sleep, and all of my insecurities and fears that I was experiencing as a young man.

When it was all over, I had a renewed sense of what I wanted to do with my life. I felt happier and more alive. I decided to breakup with my girlfriend and take up skydiving. When any of us go through a type of life-changing experience, we are forever changed and will never be the same person again!

· · · · · · ·

The past is our greatest teacher, only when we can apply our gained wisdom toward living a better life in the present. All of us are telling ourselves stories about our rationalized perception of what has happened to us and what we want to be happening in our lives. Everyone has needs, desires, fears, dreams, and beliefs. We must learn from the past and leave our incorrect actions behind, taking with us everything that is for our greatest and highest good.

> "The state of your life is nothing more than a
> reflection of your state of mind."
> — Dr. Wayne Dyer - Author of *Your Erroneous Zones*

If you don't like what you are attracting, then change the way you are acting. In order to achieve what you want in life, you must be mentally vibrating at the same level of what you want to be experiencing. Like the Law of Magnetism, we attract everything excellent and awful into our lives, through the powerful way we choose to think and feel about what is happening to us. Every thought that has inspired your decisions, every feeling that has influenced your choices, every action that has manifested into a reaction, has created the life you are living right now!

"Thought is cause. Experience is effect. If you don't like the effect in your life, you have to change the nature of your thinking."
— Marianne Williamson - Author of *A Return to Love*

• • • • • • •

LESSONS ARE EVERYWHERE… I was watching the finals of a Woman's Professional Golf Tournament at the "Kapalua Plantation Course" in Maui, Hawaii, when I witnessed something that taught me another lesson in life.

The leader teed off and hooked the ball far to the left of the fairway, into the trees. On her next shot, she drove the ball out of the rough and right into a sand trap, just to the left of the green. I watched her remain calm and focused, while she sized up her difficult situation.

The next player, who was right behind her in a close second, took her shot and wasn't very pleased with her performance. She swung her club, tore up the grass, expressed some descriptive words of frustration, and shook her head in disgust. Meanwhile, the leader in the sand trap remained positive and concentrated on the pin. She swung her club, the ball arched high into the air, it hit the green, swung to the right and fell right into the cup. The roar of the crowd was deafening. She chipped it into the hole for a two under par!

I stood there reflecting on how the game of life sometimes puts us into the same sand traps, roughs and challenging situations. And how we have a much better chance of getting out of our bad circumstances and going for the win, when we don't complain, get angry, speak words of discouragement, and choose a negative attitude.

The woman who kept a positive attitude went on to win the tournament by just one stroke and received a winner's purse of hundreds of thousands of dollars. When you change the way you look at things, the things you look at change and that gives you the advantage of the winning edge!

· · · · · · ·

"What we can or cannot do, what we consider possible or impossible, is rarely a function of our true capability. It is more likely a function of our beliefs about who we are. Whatever you hold in your mind on a consistent basis, is exactly what you will experience in your life."
— Tony Robbins - Author of *Unlimited Power*

It all began as a single drop of rain, which formed the river that created the Grand Canyon. The river flowed to the coastline, helping to fill the mighty oceans of the world. The life you are living today is the result of every drop of thought and feeling you've ever had, since you took your first breath in this world. How you choose to "Think it is," is exactly the way you will experience "How it is." The "Who" you are in your mind defines who you are in this world. Make the choice today to transform your life by the renewing of your mind by becoming more aware that everything has the power to create a good or bad, happy or sad… Grand Canyon in your life.

We see the world with our attitudes. We experience the world with our hearts. We hear the world through our spirit. We speak to the world with our emotions. Each part plays its important role in what we perceive as our reality. You are a world leader, the inspired leader of your own world.

Professional big wave surfer Greg Long puts it this way… "Every emotion, both positive and negative, is a by-product of our thoughts, and how we react to circumstances in our life is our choice alone. I am regularly put in situations that I have no control over. In doing so, I am forced to rely on my mind in order to overcome these obstacles and ride the waves I do."

· · · · · · ·

We live inside the home we construct from how we react to everything that happens to us. We pay all the bills, the insurance, and the price of repairing and maintaining it. A wise man builds up his house and a fool tears it down with his own hands. Here is a very inspirational story I found on the Internet by an unknown author…

71

THE HOUSE YOU BUILD

A very skillful carpenter was ready to retire from his construction career. He told his long time employer of his plans to leave the house-building business and live a more leisurely life with his wife and family.

The contractor was sorry to see his good worker go and asked whether he could build just one more house as a personal favor. The carpenter said, "Yes," but in time it was easy to see that his heart was not in his work. He resorted to shoddy workmanship and used inferior materials. It was an unfortunate way to end his construction career.

When the carpenter finished his work and the contractor came to inspect the house, his boss handed the front door key to the carpenter. "This is your house," he said. "My gift to you." What a shock! What a shame! If he had only known he was building his own house, he would have done it all so differently. Now he has to live in the home he chose not to build very well.

So it is with us. We build our lives in a distracted way, reacting rather than responding, willing to put up with less instead of the best. At important points, we don't give the job our best effort. Then with a shock, we look at a situation we have created and find that now we are living in the house we have built. If we had realized better, we would have done it differently.

Think of yourself as the carpenter. Think about the house you are building each and every day. As you hammer a nail, place a board, or erect a wall, build wisely. It is the only life you will ever build. Even if you live it for only one more day, that day deserves to be lived graciously and with dignity. The plaque on the wall says, "Life is a do-it-yourself project." Your life tomorrow will be the result of your thoughts, feelings, attitudes, actions, and choices you make today.

· · · · · · ·

"You are the architect of your own destiny; you are the master of your own fate. There are no limitations to what you can do, have, or be. Except the limitations you place on yourself by your own thinking."
— Brian Tracy - Author of *Create Your Own Future*

YOUR INNER VOICE… are you listening? Allow your internal spirit to speak as loud as it needs to, in order for you to hear your inner voice. You need to listen to what life is saying to you, your gut, your intuition, your instincts, your soul, and do what it is telling you. Have you ever wondered why we were created with two ears to hear, two eyes to see, but only one mouth to speak? Epictetus, a Greek sage and Stoic philosopher, who lived AD 55 to 135 AD, said, "We have two ears and one mouth, so we can listen twice as much as we speak."

· · · · · · ·

THE VOICE

There is a voice inside of you, that whispers all day long.
I feel this is right for me, I know that this is wrong.

73

No teacher, preacher, parent, friend, or wise man can decide.
What's right for you, just listen to, the voice that speaks inside.

· · · · · · ·

IN LIFE... sometimes we just keep asking the same questions over and over again, until we get the answers we want to hear! Our questions about life have so much more meaning when we look inside ourselves and find our heart-felt answers. It's all about connecting with what your inner most being is saying, shouting out the solutions from within your soul.

"Intuition is a spiritual faculty and does not explain,
but simply points the way."
— Florence Scovel Shinn - Author of
The Game of Life and How to Play It (1871-1940)

SELF-TALK... can either be positive or negative, uplifting or depressing, discouraging or encouraging. The person you talk to the most throughout your day is yourself. The average person thinks about 15,000 to 20,000 thoughts per day. If you figure that a very positive thinker may think positive thoughts 75 percent of the time, the best of us still thinks as many as 5,000 negative thoughts, each and every day. So take a moment and ask yourself this question, "Was my last thought positive or negative?"

"It's not what you say out of your mouth that determines your life. It's what you whisper to yourself that has the most power!"
— Robert T. Kiyosaki - Author of *Rich Dad, Poor Dad*

· · · · · · ·

THE CHICKEN AND THE EAGLE

Once upon a time, there was a large mountainside where an eagle's nest rested. The eagle's nest contained four large eagle eggs. One day an earthquake rocked the mountain, causing one of the eggs to roll down the mountain to a chicken farm, located in the valley below. The chickens knew they must protect and care for the eagle's egg, so an old hen volunteered to nurture and raise the large egg.

One day, the egg hatched and a beautiful eagle was born. Sadly, the eagle was raised to believe that he was nothing more than a chicken.

The eagle loved his home and family, but his spirit cried out for more. While playing a game on the farm one day, the eagle looked to the skies above and noticed a group of mighty eagles soaring in the skies. "Oh," the eagle cried, "I wish I could soar like those birds." The chickens roared with laughter, "You cannot soar with those birds. You are a chicken and chickens do not soar." The eagle continued staring at his real family up above, dreaming that he could be with them. Each time the eagle would let his dreams be known, he was told it couldn't be done. That is what the eagle learned to believe.

The eagle, after time, stopped dreaming and continued to live his life like a chicken. Finally, after a long life as a chicken, the eagle passed away.

The moral of the story... You become what you think, feel, and believe you are. So if you have ever dreamed of becoming an eagle, follow your dreams, not the words of a chicken.

· · · · · · ·

TRUST YOUR INTUITION... it is your wisest guru. Learning is more of an increased awakening, a remembering of what you intuitively already know. We all have a conscience, an inner spiritual voice, telling us what is right from wrong. The challenge is to listen to it, follow it, and use it to make the best choices and decisions. When our internal teacher is speaking, we must choose to listen to what it's saying and then do what our gut feeling is telling us to do.

"You ask me where I get my ideas. They come unsummoned directly, indirectly. I seize them with my hands out in open air, in the woods, while walking, in the silence of the nights, at dawn, excited by moods, which are translated by the poet into words, by me into tunes."
— Beethoven - Composer, "Fifth and Ninth Symphonies" (1170-1827)

We live and we learn, yet odds are you have already learned it at least once before and now it's time to put it into practice. We need to listen quietly to our inner voice and take the next right action. Then your actions will speak louder than your words.

"Right thoughts and right efforts inevitably bring about right results. You are today where your thoughts have brought you, you will be tomorrow where your thoughts take you. A man or

woman are literally what they think, their character being the complete sum of all their thoughts."
— James Allen - Author of *As a Man Thinketh* (1864-1912)

Be transformed by the renewing of your mind. The smallest change in your thinking is like a pebble dropped into a still, calm lake. The ripples of consciousness it creates spread out endlessly until they reach the shores of your inspired mind. We are always in the process of re-learning what we already know.

• • • • • • •

A CALL FOR ACTION

Be aware that at any given moment in your life, you always have a choice about the thoughts you allow into your mind. The most empowering thoughts you can have are those of peace, love, happiness, faith, gratitude, and joy.

"Your worst enemy cannot harm you as much as your own unguarded thoughts."
— Buddha - The Awakened One (563 BC-483 BC)

WHAT ARE THE NEGATIVE THOUGHTS... you would like to replace with positive ones?

1. _____.

2. _____.

3. _____.

4. _____.

5. _____.

WHAT ARE THE POSITIVE THOUGHTS... you will be replacing them with?

1. _____.

2. _____.

3. _____.

4. _____.

5. _____.

"You cannot teach a person anything, you can only
help them find it within themselves."
— Galileo - The Father of Astronomy (1564-1642)

COURSE FOUR

Having A Positive Attitude

A positive attitude is the key to happiness.

A positive attitude is more than a feeling or a state of mind. It's a commitment to deciding to choose the best possible perspective and attitude toward life. You can't complain and give thanks at the same time.

POSITIVE: Good, encouraging, confident, worthwhile, optimistic, favorable.

ATTITUDE: Viewpoint, outlook, perspective, position, reaction, opinion.

Charles Swindoll, founder of *Insight for Living* radio, explains the vital importance of our attitude… "Attitude is more important than facts. It is more important than the past, than education, than money, than circumstances, than failures, than successes, than what other people think, say, or do. I am convinced that life is 10 percent of what happens to you and 90 percent of how you react to it."

YOUR ATTITUDE WILL TAKE YOU… anywhere you want to go. Your attitude is the vehicle with which you see the world around you. A negative perspective will take you to regret, depression, sickness, fear, stress, and bad decisions. A positive attitude will take you to forgiveness, happiness, health, faith, peace, and good choices. Your attitude is either the lock or the key to enjoying your life. When you experience hardships, they don't have to turn into sinking ships! With a good attitude, hard times can transport you to an easier and better place.

> "The way to overcome negative thoughts and destructive emotions is to develop opposing, positive emotions that are stronger and more powerful."
> — The Dalai Lama - Tibetan Buddhist Leader

YOU CANNOT SERVE TWO MASTERS... constant negative thinking or persistent positive thinking. One will always be stronger than the other! Decide you are going to change your negative thoughts into positive ones before they take hold and they become harmful mindsets and strongholds. Acknowledge the source of your negative thoughts and then use what they're showing you for a positive result. If you choose not to do this... dislike becomes resentment, hate turns into depression, and being irritated affects your mental and physical health.

> "There are always two forces, warring against each other within us."
> — Paramahansa Yogananda - Author of *Autobiography of a Yogi* (1893-1952)

· · · · · · ·

TWO WOLVES

The grandson of an old and wise Cherokee Chief came to him with anger and hate toward a friend who hurt him and did him wrong. The grandfather responded by telling him this story...

"I too, at times, have felt great hate for those who have taken much from me, with no regret of what they did or how it hurt me. But harmful emotions wear you down and do not hurt your enemy. It is like taking poison and wishing the other person would die. I, like you, struggle with these feelings and have experienced them in life many times."

"It's as if there are two wolves inside of me. One wolf is evil, full of anger, fear, and death. He is filled with envy, sorrow, greed, arrogance, regret, guilt, resentment, inferiority, lies, self-pity, and false pride. The smallest thing will set him off into a fit of rage. He fights everyone, all of the time, for no good reason. He cannot think clearly because his anger and hate are so great. It is hopeless anger, for his anger will change nothing."

"The other wolf is good, full of love, serenity, hope, kindness, compassion, generosity, honesty, humility, joy, faith, and forgiveness. He lives in peace and harmony with everyone around him. He doesn't lash out and attack in anger. He only fights to protect himself from harm and to protect others in the right way."

"Sometimes it is hard to live with these two wolves inside of me, for both of them try to dominate my spirit. The same struggle is going on inside of you, and inside of every other person, too."

The young grandson thought about it for a minute and then asked his grandfather, "Which wolf will win?" The old and wise man simply replied, "The one I feed."

Which wolf are you feeding with your thoughts, feelings, actions, and reactions? Most likely, as you read these words, there is a fight going on inside of you between those same two wolves. You can tame the bad wolf that contains all your anger, sorrow, regret, and resentment, by embracing the good wolf and choosing to win this dog fight within your mind, with love and forgiveness.

. . . .

When you respond to life by giving your energy to the positive, great things happen and you get much of what you want and need in life. When you react by choosing to think and feel negative about life, too often you get what your heart doesn't desire.

The more you are grateful for what is good in your life, the more good you will be given to be grateful for. The challenge is to choose a positive attitude from thought to feeling, feeling to action, breath to breath, test to test. It makes me feel good when I say, "Life is great and getting better every day."

The spiritual activist, known only as "The Peace Pilgrim," walked across the United States for over twenty-eight years, spreading her message of love and peace… "I have chosen the positive approach. Instead of stressing the bad things which I am against, I stress the good things which I am for. Those who choose the negative approach dwell on what is wrong. Naturally, the negative approach has a detrimental effect on the person who uses it, while the positive approach has a good effect."

. . . .

82

I posted this on my Facebook page... "Your situation is only as good or as bad as you have decided to think and feel it is! Life gets instantly better when you say to yourself, "Life is great and getting better." It's all according to how you are choosing to look at things. Before you label something excellent or awful, take a look at the situation and see that it "just is." Heaven or hell, happiness or misery, the same key opens up both doors!"

This is a Facebook friend's comment to the above post... "Most of what you say is logical and I can agree. But sometimes, Rob, one cannot control situations, only react, and sometimes the situations are so grievous that it would take Jesus Christ himself to help overcome them. Everything cannot be fixed, dealt with, or banished from our lives or minds, just because we choose to be positive, spiritual, or a high road taker! Things happen, bad things happen to nice people, and sometimes things just can't be thought, meditated, prayed, and chanted away. Sometimes it continues to hurt and shapes our lives. I know you have an argument for this, but seriously, sometimes life just sucks! I'm a retired Intensive Care Unit nurse and I know how bad it can get! I am aware of how important it is to count our blessings, but sometimes I'm just human, period!"

• • • • • • •

"With a Positive Mental Attitude, failure is a learning experience, a rung on the ladder, a plateau at which to get your thoughts in order and prepare to try again."
— W. Clement Stone - Author of
Success Through A Positive Mental Attitude (1902-2002)

83

It's not the pain, loss, or suffering that teaches us; it's the healing process. When life gives you a hundred reasons to cry, give life one thousand reasons to smile. When you choose to think negatively, your whole spirit is thrown out of harmony and becomes dis-eased.

AN OPTIMISTIC OUTLOOK… sees the good in all things. *The Oxford American Dictionary* defines "optimism" as "confidence, a positive attitude, and a disposition to take a bright, hopeful view of things." A "pessimist" is defined as "an individual with a disposition to take a dark, defeatist, and negative view of things."

"The Optimist's Creed" was originally published in 1912 by Christian D. Larson in his book *Your Forces and How to Use Them*. He believed that people have tremendous latent powers, which could be harnessed for a better experience of living, with the proper optimistic attitude. This set of principles, when used, will improve your attitude and outlook on life.

· · · · · · ·

THE OPTIMIST'S CREED

I promise myself…

* To be so strong that nothing can disturb my peace of mind.

* To talk health, happiness, and prosperity to every person I meet.

* To make all my friends feel that there is something worthwhile in them.

* To look at the sunny side of everything and make my optimism come true.

* To think only of the best, to work only for the best, and to expect only the best.

* To be just as enthusiastic about the success of others, as I am about my own.

* To forget the mistakes of the past and press on to the greater achievements of the future.

* To wear a cheerful expression at all times and give a smile to every living creature I meet.

* To give so much time to improving myself, that I have no time to criticize others.

* To be too large for worry, too noble for anger, too strong for fear, and too happy to permit the presence of trouble.

* To think well of myself and to proclaim this fact to the world, not in loud words, but in great deeds.

* To live in the faith that the whole world is on my side, so long as I am true to the best that is in me.

· · · · · · ·

"Optimism is a happiness magnet. If you stay positive, good things and good people will be drawn to you."
— Mary Lou Retton - 1984 Olympic Gold Medal Gymnast

START YOUR DAY BY PRETENDING... that it's going to be an awesome day, and you will have a great day. Too many people say, "Have a great day" to others and choose not to have one themselves! You get to decide what emotions, behaviors, and responses you will choose today. By choosing to think and feel positive about things, you create your "I'm having a great day in every way, no matter what is happening to me, throughout the day" attitude toward life.

Choose to spend more time with people who are positive, supportive, uplifting, and encouraging. We're all influenced by the people we talk to, listen to, and socialize with. Films, music, books, TV, and the media all have a positive or negative effect on us. Choose wisely what goes into your mind, for it then goes to the heart and soul for action.

· · · · · · ·

HOME REFLECTS THE HEART

There is an ancient story that tells of a young man who traveled to an oasis next to a town. He tied up his camel and approached an old man. He asked, "What kind of people live in this place?" The old man replied, "What kind of people live in the place where you are coming from?" The young man got all excited and huffy saying, "They are all a group of selfish and wicked people! I am happy I have left there." The old man answered, "You will find the same kind of people living here."

That same day, another young man approached the oasis to drink water from its well, and seeing the old man, he asked, "What kind of people live in this place?" The old man answered with the same question, "What kind of people live in the place where you are coming from?" The young man enthusiastically answered, "A magnificent group of people. They are honest, friendly, generous, kind, and it hurts very much to have left them." The old man replied, "You will find the same kind of people living here."

A man who had heard both conversations asked the old man, "How is it possible to give two different answers to the same question?" To which the old man answered, "Each person carries with him in his heart and mind, the power to create the environment where he lives. The young man who didn't like anything about where he lived before will most likely not find anything new or different here. He will have brought with him the reality he will create in this new place. The one who found only friends and good things where he lived has the power to find the same things here. Because, to tell the truth, your mental attitude is the only thing in your life over which you can maintain absolute control."

When you choose to have an optimistic outlook, you'll find the true richness in life. If you look within, you will know that you possess a great strength to find the good in all things. May you always find an oasis of love, peace, and happiness!

· · · · · · ·

The optimist and the pessimist each lives his or her life in completely different ways. Pessimists use worry as a form of praying for what they don't want to happen. Optimists use a positive attitude and outlook on life, as a form of praying for what they know can happen. Either way, they both get what they ask for.

"The pessimist complains about the wind. The optimist expects it to change. The realist adjusts the sails."
— William A. Ward - Author of *Fountains of Faith* (1921-1994)

Your perception, awareness, and opinion of the mistakes, wrong decisions, and problems in your life will either make you happy and glad or depressed and mad. How you think, feel, and believe determines whether you have a healthy or an unhealthy living experience. The problems in your life don't define you. Instead, your responses to these challenges will determine who you are, and who you are becoming today, tomorrow, and for the rest of your life.

Bad things will occasionally be happening to us. Just turn on the news and experience the next tragedy and hear about all of the bad stuff happening in your area and the world! Our challenge is to find the good in each problem and to use it to contribute to the positive solutions in our lives.

"Things turn out best for the people who make the best of the way things turn out."
— Art Linkletter - TV Show Host (1912-2010)

If your house burns down, is your entire life now destroyed or will you reconstruct a better future from the ruins? The course of your life is determined by how you choose to think and feel about the rubble that remains long after the fire is out. If you look with a grateful heart and a positive attitude, you will find opportunity, hope, and beauty within the ashes. This will not be easy, yet all of your other options will be much harder on you!

Your life isn't about the good or bad experiences you'll have over the years. Everyone has both good and bad, happy and sad. What matters is what you do with your thoughts and feelings about what happens to you in life. What we focus on increases and we get more of it. So if you concentrate your thoughts and feelings on the good, things get better. If you choose to focus on the bad, things get worse! It's that simple and it is as powerful as the law of gravity.

> "Believe it or not, if it weren't for your so-called issues, problems, and challenges, there would be no other way you could become even happier, cooler, and more enlightened than you have ever been before."
> — Mike Dooley - Author of *Notes from the Universe*

· · · · · · ·

THREE HAIRS

There once was a woman who woke up one morning, looked in the mirror, and noticed she had only three hairs on her head. "Well," she said, "I think I'll braid my hair today." So she did and she had a wonderful day.

The next day she woke up, looked in the mirror, and saw that she had only two hairs on her head. "Hmmm," she said, "I

89

think I'll part my hair down the middle today." So she did and she had a great day.

The next day she woke up, looked in the mirror, and noticed that she had only one hair on her head. "Well," she said, "Today I'm going to wear my hair in a pony tail." So she did, and she had a fun, fun day.

The next day she woke up, looked in the mirror, and noticed that there wasn't a single hair on her head. "Yay!" she exclaimed. "I don't have to fix my hair today!"

Attitude is everything. Be kinder than necessary, for everyone you meet is fighting some kind of battle. Live simply, love generously, care deeply, and speak kindly.

· · · · · · ·

Positivity is contagious, yet so is negativity. Negativity spreads like a virus, the flu, and has the potential to turn into an epidemic of unhealthy feelings. There is only one cure for this sickness of the heart, mind, and soul... and that is love, forgiveness and a healthy inspired emotional change. Anxiety, worry, stress, and depression can't give you the strength you'll need to overcome your challenging circumstances. These emotional choices only add weakness, and suffering to a situation that isn't so good to begin with! We need to use the bad news to create good news within us. Positive thinking and an optimistic outlook are at the forefront of every good thing that happens.

If you look at the problems in your life, each as a grain of sand, you will see they are part of the beautiful beaches of life. It would be a shame to allow some bad sand to stop you from having an enjoyable and relaxing day at the ocean! Is a little sand wearing away at your positive attitude and heart-felt gratitude?

"Dwelling on the negative, simply contributes to its power."
— Shirley MacLaine - Actress, Author of *Out On A Limb*

My Facebook friends and followers are always commenting on my inspirational posts and saying to me, "You have such a positive and optimistic outlook on life." And my response is always, "I tried a bad attitude, a negative outlook, and a depressed response to what happens to me in life, and that just left me unhappy, unhealthy, and with a very negative living experience. So I came to a place where I had to make a choice, and I chose a positive and optimistic attitude. It makes all the difference in my world. Try it… you'll like it!"

. . . .

A CALL FOR ACTION

WHAT THINGS DO YOU HAVE IN YOUR LIFE THAT ARE GOOD?

1. _____.

2. _____.

3. _____.

4. _____.

5. _____.

"See the positive possibilities. Redirect the substantial energy of your frustration and turn it into positive, effective, and unstoppable determination."
— Ralph Marston - Author of *The Daily Motivator*

WHAT THINGS DO YOU HAVE IN YOUR LIFE THAT ARE NOT AS GOOD AS YOU WOULD LIKE THEM TO BE?

1. _____.

2. _____.

3. _____.

4. _____.

5. _____.

"Once you replace negative thoughts with positive ones, you'll start having positive results."
— Willie Nelson - Singer, Musician, Actor

WHAT THINGS CAN YOU DO TO CHANGE YOUR NEGATIVES INTO POSITIVES, YOUR PROBLEMS INTO POSSIBILITIES, AND YOUR CHALLENGES INTO OPPORTUNITIES?

1. _____.

2. _____.

3. _____.

4. _____.

5. _____.

COURSE FIVE

Feeling Your Emotions

Emotions are feelings in motion.

All of our emotions, thoughts and feelings, come from either love or fear. Within love comes faith, in fear is doubt, within love comes happiness and in fear is anxiety.

How you think and feel about your life, is your life! It brings you everything you want and don't want. Take a look deep inside yourself and ask, "What excuses and fears are causing the pain and tears that are holding me back in my life? What worries and doubts have created my drought, where there should be a river of flowing faith?"

There is no intimacy without vulnerability. When you risk being rejected, dare to be scared, take the chance of failing and being disappointed, that is when you open up the door to courage, faith, confidence, and the real-life experiences worth having! Too many of us numb our true emotions so we don't feel too much, think too much or open ourselves up too much, thus avoiding having to be truly honest with ourselves and others!

"I learned that courage was not the absence of fear, but the triumph over it! After climbing a great hill, one only finds that there are many more hills to climb."
— Nelson Mandela - South African President (1918-2013)

The events in our lives shape us, yet our choices and decisions are what define us. We are all self-made individuals, doing what we feel is the best thing for us. There can be no blaming others for what you don't like in your life. There will always be three people involved in everything you do… me, myself and I. You can't go anywhere without taking yourself with you.

We pay a high price when we trade the power of love, for the love of power. We exchange the power of helping for the power of controlling. We trade humility for pride, peace for anger, happiness for depression, kindness for hate, gratitude for complaining, faith for fear, and hope for despair. Yet it's so encouraging to know that if you're no longer satisfied with your purchase, there is a 100 percent return policy!

Who is in control of your emotions? No one can make you feel, "This way" or "That way," unless you give them the permission to do so. People affect us in either a positive or negative way and then we decide how we choose to feel in that given moment. Nothing and nobody can ruin your day without your consent, permission or agreement!

"The greatest revolution of our generation is the discovery that human beings, by changing the inner attitudes of their minds, can change the outer aspects of their lives."
—William James - Psychologist (1842-1910)

Make a decision that you won't allow what people say and do to determine how you think and feel about yourself and the world around you. You are the only one who is either in control or out of control of your self-created emotions. Make the choice not to rent out any space in your head to other people's unhealthy opinions.

"Never react emotionally to criticism. Analyze yourself to determine whether it is justified. If it is, correct yourself. Otherwise, go on about your business."
— Norman Vincent Peale - Author of *Enthusiasm Makes the Difference* (1898-1993)

Every time someone bothers me or has a strong opinion about what I am doing, I stop and ask myself, "What is this telling me about myself, and how can I learn and grow from it?" The answers aren't always perfectly clear or comfortable, yet when I do this, it always helps me put things into a more loving perspective.

Jim Morrison, legendary singer and songwriter for The Doors, says, "People are afraid of their own reality, their feelings most of all. People talk about how great love is, but love hurts. Feelings are disturbing. People are taught that pain is evil and dangerous. How can they deal with love, if they're afraid to feel? Pain is meant to wake us up."

· · · · · · ·

I had an 11:30 a.m. doctor's appointment today. I didn't feel like going, yet I knew I should. I had to stop what I was doing, get ready, and wound up hitting heavy traffic on the way there!

When I arrived at the office on time, the receptionist apologized for running behind schedule and told me I would have to wait five or ten minutes. Well, five turned into ten, ten into twenty, twenty into an hour. I finally came to the realization that the only thing I was ultimately in control of was how I was responding to my potentially very irritating situation.

So I asked the receptionist what was going on, and as a result, I decided to reschedule for another day. I left there feeling good about how I handled my challenging circumstance. I had multiple opportunities to allow myself to get upset and impatient. Why shouldn't I? I was on time and should expect things to go the way I wanted them to! Yet is that the way life really is?

Real life should be about choosing to be understanding, patient, and pleasant about what we can't control. A calm and positive attitude changed what could have been a very upsetting experience for me, into one of learning, strengthening, and growth.

We act out, express, and manifest in our outer life, what we are thinking and feeling in our inner life. No one is perfect. We all have a measure of bad that comes with our goodness, conflict with our peace, dislike with our love, a little suffering with our joy. With each step we take, we can choose to move forward with the right attitude or backwards with the wrong way of thinking, feeling, and doing.

"Like a small grain of sand which irritates the oyster to yield the pearl, the person in our lives that creates the greatest level of discomfort, is also the one who has the most to teach us."
— Eckhart Tolle - Author of *The Power of Now*

By the way... I wasn't always like this. It was nice to see that some things have changed within myself. We never know how we really are, until we're tested by getting the chance to find out who we have become. Life is an educational process. We are all learning how to be in control of our emotions, instead of the situation having emotional control over us! Can you relate to my story?

> "If we're growing, we're always going to be out
> of our comfort zone."
> —John Maxwell - Author of *Motivated to Succeed*

· · · · · · ·

People build too many walls and not enough bridges. In a pile of old papers inside a dresser drawer, I found this poem handwritten by a father to his daughter...

BURNING BRIDGES

I've burned a lot of bridges in my time,
Left a trail of ashes, through the years.
Backed myself into a solid wall,
And been to blame for more than half my tears.
Tripped on pride and fell upon my face,
Bitten off much more than I could chew.
Detoured over many needless miles,
And even missed the boat a time or two.

· · · · · · ·

When you choose to feel disappointed about things not being the way you hoped and expected they could, would, and should have been, you are robbed of the positive energy you need to transform your who, what, and how into your good, better, and best life now!

· · · · · · ·

LEAVING THE CITY OF REGRET

by Larry Harp

I had not really planned on taking a trip this time of year, and yet I found myself packing rather hurriedly. This trip was going to be unpleasant, and I knew in advance that no real good would come of it. I'm talking about my annual *"Guilt Trip."* I got tickets to fly there on *"Wish I Had"* airlines. It was an extremely short flight. I got my baggage, which I could not check. I chose to carry it myself all the way. It was weighed down with a thousand memories of what might have been.

No one greeted me as I entered the terminal at the *Regret City International Airport.* I say international because people from all over the world come to this dismal town. As I checked into the *Last Resort Hotel,* I noticed that it would be hosting the year's most important event, the *Annual Pity Party.* I wasn't going to miss that great social occasion. Many of the town's leading citizens would be there.

First, there would be the *Done family; You Know, Should Have, Would Have, and Could Have.* Then came the *I Had family.*

98

You probably know old *Wish* and his clan. Of course, the *Opportunities* would be present, *Missed and Lost*. The biggest family would be the *Yesterdays*. There are far too many of them to count, but each one would have a very sad story to share. Then *Shattered Dreams* would surely make an appearance. And *It's Their Fault* would regale us with stories (excuses), about how things had failed in his life, and each story would be loudly applauded by *Don't Blame Me* and *I Couldn't Help It*.

Well, to make a long story short, I went to this depressing party knowing that there would be no real benefit in doing so. And, as usual, I became very depressed. But as I thought about all of the stories of failures brought back from the past, it occurred to me that all of this trip and subsequent *Pity Party* could be cancelled by me!

I truly started to realize that I did not have to be there. I didn't have to be depressed. One thing kept going through my mind, "I can't change yesterday, but I do have the power to make today, a wonderful day. I can be happy, joyous, fulfilled, encouraged, as well as encouraging." Knowing this, I left the *City of Regret* immediately and left no forwarding address. Am I sorry for mistakes I've made in the past? Yes, but there is no physical way to undo them!

So, if you're planning a trip back to the *City of Regret*, please cancel your reservations now. Instead, take a trip to a place called *Starting Again*. I liked it so much that I have now taken up permanent residence there. My neighbors, the *I Forgive Myselfs* and the *New Starts*, are very helpful. By the way, you don't have to carry around heavy baggage, because the load is lifted from your shoulders upon arrival. God Bless you in finding this great town. If you can find it and it's in your own heart, please look me up. I live on *I Can Do It Street*!

. . . .

Guilt, shame, regret, and remorse, are like raging rivers that cannot be dammed up. You must release the waters and allow the negative feelings to flow out and away from your life, while letting the currents take you to a new place of happiness and healing. Don't allow your emotions to pull you down and drown you into the depths of darkness.

Time heals all wounds, and now is the time and place to receive your transformation into health and well being. Your emotional breakdown is a chance to rebuild yourself in a stronger and better way. Live, laugh, and smile again. Leave the past behind. Choose to release the pain and embrace the flowing waters of peace, faith, hope, and love.

> "Others are only mirrors of you. You cannot love or hate something about another, unless it reflects something you love or hate about yourself."
> — Cherie Carter-Scott - Author of *If Love Is a Game, These Are the Rules*

When you hate or choose anger, you become it! Evil hurts the perpetrator as much as the victim. Love blesses and changes everyone, everything, and the entire situation around you. Love may not stop hate and anger from happening, yet it will always stop it from gaining final power over you and others. When you choose to add love and kindness, instead of more stress and negativity to the situation, your world becomes a better place to live.

"Anger is like a storm. When you feel it coming, think of the person triggering this emotion with mindfulness, so you can see they are unhappy and suffering. Then you'll feel motivated to say or do something to help the other person suffer less. When compassion appears, anger is deleted."
— Thich Nhat Hanh – Buddhist Monk, Author of *Your True Home*

Dissatisfaction is the gloomy feeling we create, after taking action and not getting the results we wanted. Since we did not get the positive emotion of satisfaction, we choose to create a negative response within ourselves. The feelings of disappointment weren't given to us, we gave them to ourselves! The results did not create the bad feelings, I did! Only I can make myself feel, "Any way I choose."

· · · · · · ·

THE CRACKED POT

Many years ago, there was a Water-Bearer who had two large pots that he carried across his neck, hanging from the end of a pole. Both pots were created to be able to carry a full measure of water. One of the pots had a crack in it, while the other pot was made perfect.

The Flawless Pot was proud of delivering a full portion of water at the end of the long walk from the stream to the master's house. The Cracked Pot felt bad about always arriving half full. This caused the Water-Bearer to be able to deliver only one and a half pots of water each day. The Cracked Pot was embarrassed about its flaws and imperfections, while always feeling guilty for only accomplishing half of what it was capable of doing.

After years of what it perceived to be bitter failure and disappointment, the Cracked Pot spoke to the Water-Bearer one day by the stream. "I am ashamed of myself, and I want to apologize to you." "Why?" asked the Water-Bearer. "What are you ashamed of?" "I can only deliver half of what I am capable of because this crack in my side leaks water all the way back to your master's house. Because of my flaws you do all of this work and you don't get the full credit for your efforts," the Cracked Pot said.

The Water-Bearer felt sorry for the broken and depressed pot, and in his compassion said, "As we return to the master's house, I want you to notice the beautiful flowers growing along the path." As they went up the hill, the Cracked Pot took notice of the sun warming the beautiful flowers on his side of the path, and this seemed to cheer him up. But at the end of the trail, half of its water had leaked out, and so again the Cracked Pot apologized for its lack of performance.

The Water-Bearer said to the pot, "Did you notice there were flowers only on your side of the path, and there were none on the Flawless Pot's side?" This is because I have always known about your flaw. And because of my love and appreciation for you, I took advantage of it. I planted flower seeds on your side of the path, and every day while we walked back from the stream, you have been watering them through the crack in your side. For two years I have been able to pick these beautiful flowers to decorate my master's table. Without you being just the way you are, we would not have this beauty to grace my master's house.

Each of us is a Cracked Pot in one way or another, yet there is no limit to the amount of beauty we can create. We can inflict so much pain and suffering upon ourselves by thinking about what we are not and how we wish things could, would, and should be. Yet it is only when we are willing to love and accept ourselves just the way we are that our lives become filled with joy, peace and happiness.

• • • • • • •

"You have never, not for one moment, been off your path.
And you have no reason whatsoever to feel any embarrassment
or discomfort about where you are at this stage in your life.
You are powerfully on your path and you are just
beginning the best part of your life."
— Esther Hicks - Inspirational Speaker, Spiritual Teacher

Compassion is the understanding of the sufferings and feelings within ourselves and others. It's the emotion we feel in response to another's pain. Compassion is the sympathy, concern, warmth and tenderness for the misfortunes of other people and things. It is considered to be among the greatest of all virtues.

• • • • • • •

Saint Francis of Assisi said it all in his thirteenth century prayer…

Where there is hatred, let me bring love.
Where there is wrong, may I bring the spirit of forgiveness.
Where there is discord, may I bring harmony.
Where there is error, may I bring truth.
Where there is doubt, may I bring faith.
Where there is despair, may I bring hope.
Where there is darkness, may I bring light.
Where there is sadness, may I bring joy.

Oh Divine Master, Grant that I may not so much seek to be consoled, as to console. To be understood, as to understand. To be loved, as to love. For it is in giving, that we receive. It is in pardoning, that we are pardoned. And it is in dying, that we are born to eternal life.

· · · · · · ·

"Fake it until you make it" is a great saying! The concept is simple. Most people think we act because of how we are feeling. Human behavioral research now shows that we more often feel because of the way we act. So when you want to change your emotions, then act the way you want to feel.

For example, if you are feeling low and want to be happy, then find something that will make you act happy, and after repeated actions, you will feel happy. If you are stuck inside a complaining negative attitude, think grateful and positive thoughts long enough until your perspective changes into a positive attitude.

You think, feel, and act according to what you focus on. So change your thought and feeling actions and everything will soon change for the better. When there is no new action, there will be no changed reaction or renewed state of desired emotions. Try it… it really is that simple!

"Smile; it's the key that fits the lock of everybody's heart."
—Anthony J. D'Angelo - CVO of Collegiate Empowerment

COURSE SIX

Finding Happiness

Happiness is an inside job.

The New Oxford Dictionary defines "Happiness" as a feeling or the showing of pleasure, having a sense of satisfaction with a person, arrangement, or situation. A place where success, contentment, and enjoyment is obtained. A state of mind that produces the emotions of gratitude, wellbeing, merriment, exhilaration, and good spirits.

> "Happiness is the meaning and the purpose of life,
> the whole aim of human existence."
> —Aristotle - Greek Philosopher, Scientist (384 BC-322 BC)

I THINK THIS MAY BE ONE OF THE MOST WIDELY BELIEVED LIES ON THE PLANET... "When I get what I want, I'll be happy." You believe that some-thing, or some-one, some-day will make you happy. We always need to remind ourselves to be content and happy right now. Not tomorrow, today! There's no better time to be happy than in this very moment. And always remember that nobody is happy all of the time.

> "Just because something made you happy in the past,
> doesn't mean you have to keep it forever."
> —Dr. Melva Green - Psychiatrist, Behavioral Therapist

Anything we think we need to have in order for us to be happy will only make us feel good for a while and then fade away. These things will produce pleasure that comes and goes, and excitement that will leave when we grow used to it.

LOOKING FOR HAPPINESS... Many of us are trying to find our happiness in people, places, and things. It's tempting to think we'll be happy when something or someone outside of ourselves makes us happy. We say to ourselves, "If I only had more money, a nicer car, a better relationship, a bigger house, nicer clothes, more stuff, and a better job, I would be happy." We convince ourselves that life will be happier when we get married or divorced, take a vacation, lose weight, get what we want, get back what we lost, or when they do this or they do that!

> "The foolish seek happiness in the distance,
> the wise grow it under their feet."
> — James Oppenheim - Author of *The Book of Self* (1882-1932)

· · · · · · ·

THE FIELD OF JOY

There were many good hearted people looking for happiness in a field called "Life." In this field were many rocks lying among the dirt, weeds, and thorns. Some rocks presented themselves as problems and obstacles, while others as pain and difficulties.

In the middle of the field, there was a pile of rocks that were so big and sharp, you couldn't get through or over them, no matter how hard you tried! Yet lying among the same rocks, was another group of stones that formed a smooth path, leading to feelings of joy, cheerfulness, love, and uplifting delight.

The people searched long and hard, looking everywhere and trying everything to find happiness. After pushing over every rock and digging in the earth around them, they became discouraged, frustrated, and exhausted from their strenuous and unproductive work.

After resting and thinking for a while, they decided to look for happiness in all of the places where they never thought of looking before. First, they let go of the past and began looking behind the problem rocks, where they found opportunities to learn, grow, and change. They discovered under the big and jagged rocks, small things to be grateful for and chances to help others find happiness and joy. Along the smoother path of stones, they came upon the realization that all things good and bad lead back to the heart, where true happiness and love can only be found.

They each, in their own way, understood that before they began searching for happiness, it was already inside of them, wanting to become a part of their daily life. They learned that happiness doesn't come from things, that is called enjoyment and pleasure. That good and bad, happy or sad, life unfolds according to the way we choose to see it. That when you decide to look behind and under the rocks in your "Field of Life," you'll find inspiration and solutions, among the situations and problems that look and feel like hard and heavy rocks! They discovered that sometimes you have to dig through the dirt, in order to find your emotional diamonds and gems! — RW

· · · · · · ·

Real and lasting happiness isn't found in things! They will never be the true source of this self-created emotion. Your happiness has always been and will always be found, right inside of you. Most people will only be as happy as they decide to be.

"Life, liberty, and the pursuit of happiness. The U.S. Constitution doesn't guarantee happiness, only your right to pursue it."

— Benjamin Franklin - Politician, Inventor (1706-1790)

START MAKING YOUR OWN HAPPINESS A PRIORITY... If you can't find happiness on your own, how can you expect someone or something to give it to you? Choose to work on yourself, instead of trying to make other people responsible for your happiness. Take off your "I'm fine" mask, take a risk, and tell people what you are honestly thinking and feeling inside of you. Decide to show the real you, instead of the person you think others want you to be. If you don't value yourself, you won't be a value to anyone else. We are all a victim of "identity theft," when we are not living as our "true self."

"As long as anyone believes that their ideal and purpose is outside of them, they will go outside themselves and seek fulfillment where it cannot be found. They will look for solutions and answers at every point except where they can be found inside of themselves."

— Erich Fromm - German Psychologist (1900-1980)

EVERYTHING IS THE KEY TO HAPPINESS… The door is never locked; it's always open. There are many doors you can enter through and many ways to walk through them. Happiness isn't just about feeling good and experiencing bliss, fun, pleasure, or enjoyment. Happiness is a learned habit. Each of us is "who" and "what" we are today because of the happy or sad thoughts we permit to occupy our mind.

In her book *The How of Happiness: A New Approach to Getting the Life You Want*, Sonja Lyubomirsky explains… "Enjoying a real increase in your own happiness is in fact attainable, if you are prepared to do the work. Backed by the results of our research, 40 percent is that part of our happiness which is in our power to change, through how we act and how we think."

Positive Psychology studies show that 50 percent of our happiness comes from within us, even down to our DNA. Ten percent comes from circumstances, income, social status, age, where you live, job, health, and 40 percent is unaccounted for and is totally created by our self. Things we can practice on a regular basis are love, forgiveness, a healthy diet, exercise, positive thinking, keeping a gratitude journal, and being happy no matter what!

> "The secret of happiness is in knowing how to enjoy the
> greatest pleasures of life, without forgetting the little
> things we have in our reach."
> — Paulo Coelho - Author of *The Alchemist*

TO GAIN HAPPINESS… you must learn to enjoy what you already have and never be afraid of losing it! The only reason I have to be unhappy, is if I choose to mourn over the things I have lost or to focus on what I want and haven't gotten yet! Happiness isn't about getting what you want; it's about wanting what you have and being grateful for it. It's not how much you have, it's all about how you think about what you have, that produces happiness or discontent, gratitude, or wanting. After all, life is not about things. It's all about how much love I have in my life… love for myself, love for others, and my choice to love life.

True happiness brings with it more riches than all the money in the world. There is no greater loss than the loss of my happiness, and all of the money and stuff in the world can't give it back to me!

"A happy person is not a person in a certain set of circumstances, but rather a person with a certain set of attitudes."
— Hugh Downs - TV News Anchor

• • • • • • •

THE SACK

A boy came upon a frowning man, walking along the road to town. "What's wrong?" he asked. The man held up a tattered bag and moaned, "All that I own in this world barely fills this miserable, wretched sack." "Too bad," said the boy, and with that, he snatched the bag from the man's hands and ran down the road with it!

Having lost everything, the man burst into tears and more miserable than before, continued walking. Meanwhile, the boy quickly ran around the bend and placed the man's sack in the middle of the road where he would come upon it. When the man saw his bag sitting in the road before him, he laughed with joy and shouted, "My sack, I thought I'd lost you!" Watching through the bushes, the boy chuckled, "Well, that's one way to make someone happy!"

· · · · · · ·

"Happiness can be found even in the darkest of times,
if one only remembers to turn on the light."
— *Harry Potter and the Prisoner of Azkaban* movie 2004

I went to the mailbox and pulled out my Netflix mailer with the DVD *Happy* inside. It came on the same day I was writing this chapter, so I put it into my DVD player right away. The film explores the secrets behind our most valued emotion, "Happiness." As I watched the movie, this is some of the inspired information I wrote down... To be happy is a man or woman's greatest desire and pursuit in life. When you ask people "What do you want out of life?" you would think most people would answer money, sex, a big house, a new car, and lots of stuff. Yet the most common answer is "to be happy."

"Plenty of people miss their share of happiness, not because
they never found it, but because they didn't stop to enjoy it."
— William Feather – *The William Feather Magazine* (1889-1981)

The United States is ranked twenty-fifth in the world for cultures that are studied in the "World Happiness Rankings." America has the most suicides and over 17 million people a year are diagnosed with clinical depression, more than any other country in the world.

"Even a happy life cannot be without a measure of darkness,
and the word 'happy' would lose its meaning,
if it were not balanced by sadness."
— Carl Jung - Swiss Psychiatrist (1875-1961)

The film *Happy* documented a very special place called Bhutan, which is an ancient culture secluded high in the Himalayas, just south of Tibet. Their government has made a commitment to make their countries' number one goal "The pursuit of happiness." The people feel that humanity needs a higher goal for development and theirs is the concept of "Gross National Happiness," instead of "Gross National Product."

"Happy people do not demand a lot from the world, because their happiness proceeds from a place deeper than the world can touch."
— Alan Cohen - Author of *How Good Can It Get*

FINDING HAPPINESS… You're only as happy as you choose to be. You are totally responsible for making yourself happy or unhappy, according to how you react or respond to the world inside and outside of you. Your choices lead you up the path to your own front door! It isn't the place where you live that makes it a happy home; it's the person living inside the house. There is no need to search for happiness; it's all around you. It is your job to see it, receive it, feel it, be it, and share it.

"Happiness held is the seed, happiness shared is the flower."
— John Harrigan - Author of *Empty Dreams, Empty Pockets*

• • • • • • •

IF YOU WANT HAPPINESS

A young student was taking a walk with his professor, who was affectionally called, "The students' friend." As they went along, they saw a pair of old shoes lying in the path, which belonged to a poor man who was working in a field close by. The student turned to the professor saying, "Let's play a trick on this man. We will hide his shoes, and hide ourselves behind those bushes, and wait to see his confusion when he cannot find them."

"My young friend," answered the professor. "We should never amuse ourselves at the expense of the poor. But you are rich, and may give yourself a much greater pleasure by means of this poor man."

"Put a coin in each shoe, and then we will hide ourselves and watch how this affects him." The student did so and they both placed themselves behind the bushes close by. The poor man soon finished his work, and came across the field to the path, where he had left his coat and shoes.

While slipping his foot into one of his shoes, he felt something hard and he stooped down to feel what it was. He reached inside and found the coin. His face was filled with astonishment and joy. He gazed upon the coin, turned it over and around, and looked at it again and again. He then looked all around him, but no person was to be seen. He now put the money into his pocket and proceeded to put on the other shoe. He was doubly surprised at finding yet another miraculous coin.

His feelings overcame him as he fell upon his knees, looked up to heaven, and uttered aloud a heartfelt thanksgiving in which he spoke of his sick wife and hungry children; and how this timely bounty from some unknown hand would save them from perishing!

The student stood there deeply affected and his eyes filled with tears. "Now," said the professor, "aren't you much better pleased than if you had played your intended trick on this poor man?"

The youth replied, "You have taught me a lesson which I will never forget." I feel now the truth of these words which I never understood before, "It is more blessed to give, than to receive."

· · · · · · ·

"Sometimes when I'm not feeling so happy, I do something to make someone else happy, then I find I'm suddenly feeling happy again."
— Karen Salmansohn - Author of *How To Be Happy, Dammit*

Marcus Aurelius is the Roman Emperor portrayed in the hit movie *Gladiator*. He is considered to be the last of the "Five Good Emperors" and one of the most important Stoic philosophers. Over 2000 years ago, he wrote this simple self-help piece of advice... "I have seen the beauty of good and have recognized that the happiness of your life depends upon the quality of your thoughts."

The ancient egyptians believed that when their souls got to the entrance of "The After Life," they were asked two questions. The first question was "Have you found happiness in life?" The second question was "Has your life brought happiness to others?" Their answers determined whether or not they were admitted into paradise. What would your answer be... Yes or No?

BEING HAPPY... We all want to have a successful, happy, and love-filled life. Happiness is a state of being. It is never stopping to think if you are happy or not, because you just are. It never means that everything is perfect. It means you've decided to look beyond the imperfections and have chosen to be happy, regardless of your circumstances. Happiness is an attitude. It takes the same amount of effort to make yourself unhappy as it does to be happy. It's all a matter of choice! Love and happiness is the whole aim of life and the reason for our human existence. When you choose to be unhappy, you die before you die, one joyless moment at a time!

> "I've learned from experience that the greater part of our
> happiness or misery depends on our character and
> not on our circumstances."
> — Martha Washington - Wife of Pres. George Washington (1731-1802)

· · · · · · ·

SUGGESTIONS FOR BEING HAPPY

✴ Free your heart from hatred.

✴ Free your mind from worries.

✴ Live simply, give more, expect less.

✴ Be grateful for everything.

✴ Love and forgive yourself.

· · · · · · ·

The great comedian Groucho Marx explained happiness this way… "I, not events, have the power to make me happy or unhappy today. I can choose which it shall be. Yesterday is dead, tomorrow hasn't arrived yet. I have just one day, today, and I'm going to be happy in it."

. . . .

A CALL FOR ACTION

Your Happiness List

Be aware of the level of your happiness and unhappiness, and what your mind is full of. The secret to happiness is being content in all of life's situations and conditions. Choose to be happy in lack as well as in prosperity, sickness, and in health, and when things are going great, as well as when they're not going so well.

"Happiness is not the absence of problems,
but the ability to deal with them."
— Charles Louis de Montesquieu - French Politician (1689-1755)

ARE YOU HAPPY?… Answering this question honestly can sometimes be very difficult! Is happiness the absence of depression and suffering? Is it fun, pleasure, or enjoyment? For some it is based on how much money they have and their success in their careers. For others it's all about the love relationships and friendships they are experiencing. So, happiness is not only self-created, but also self-defined.

Does money buy you happiness or does happiness make your money more enjoyable while spending it? We have all heard the saying, "Money can't buy you happiness." Yet recent studies show there is a direct connection between money and happiness. If you can't pay your bills or afford food and are just plain broke, and money comes into your life, there is a dramatic increase in your happiness based on the decrease of financial stress.

> "It isn't easy to find happiness in ourselves,
> and it is not possible to find it elsewhere."
> — Agnes Repplier – Essayist, "In Pursuit of Laughter" (1858-1950)

At the same time, when you study a person who has all of his needs taken care of, has a normal amount of debt and financial stress, and you give him more money, his increased happiness in not very dramatic. Studies show that the difference between making $50,000 and a million dollars a year, creates more ability to buy more stuff and do more things and doesn't necessarily bring an increase of happiness.

Denis Waitley, self-help author and inspirational speaker, expressed it this way… "Success is not the key to happiness. Happiness is the key to success. If you love what you are doing, you will be successful. Happiness cannot be traveled to, owned, earned or worn. It is the spiritual experience of living every minute with love, grace and gratitude."

The "Hedonic Treadmill" states that whatever level of wealth or material abundance you have, you get used to it and always

119

want more. Thus, money can't buy lasting happiness, only temporary gratification and pleasure. Does your stuff really make you happy or does your happiness make the difference in how much you like your stuff?

"You can easily find people who are ten times as rich at sixty, as they were at twenty. But not one of them will tell you that they are ten times as happy."
— George Bernard Shaw - Author of *Immaturity* (1856-1950)

Have you ever wondered what made people happy 2000… 1000… 500 or 100 years ago? What created their happiness before TV, movies, jewelry, cars, big houses, convenience products, cell phones, computers, electronics, video games, drugs, fame, and fortune? If material things were the answer to having a meaningful and happy life, we would all live in a mall.

"Am I happy?" If your answer is "Yes, I am happy," then you should know why. If your response is "No, I am not happy," then ask yourself why?

WHAT MAKES YOU HAPPY?

1. _____.

2. _____.

3. _____.

4. _____.

5. _____.

We all have two basic goals in life.

1. Intrinsic goals, which are inside of ourselves such as personal growth, finding meaning and purpose in life, and happiness.

2. Extrinsic goals, which are outside of ourselves such as money, image, status, possessions, power, prestige, and relationships. Research shows that committing random acts of kindness, increases your well-being and happiness levels.

> "Happiness is when what you think, what you say,
> and what you do, are in harmony."
> — Gandhi - Political Philosopher (1869-1948)

After many years of research, studies have found that people who focused on extrinsic goals or goals outside of themselves were less satisfied with their lives, more stressed, depressed, anxious, had less vitality, and over-all poorer health. People who were focused more on intrinsic goals, or things inside themselves, were happier, healthier, calmer, had more inner peace, more energy, an increased sense of purpose, and lived longer.

Life is all about the adding up of pluses and minuses. A happy life is the result of seeing things as a plus, no matter what the situation adds up to! These two goals, intrinsic and extrinsic, are in direct opposition to each other. Happiness is found in the balance, somewhere in between the two.

WHAT THINGS ARE MAKING YOU UNHAPPY?

1. _____.

2. _____.

3. _____.

4. _____.

5. _____.

> "I never met an unhappy person who was grateful."
>
> — Deb Scott – Author of *The Sky is Green and The Grass is Blue*

As you get older you find out, that true happiness is not in how much you make or how many degrees you have or how big your house is or how fancy your car is. Happiness is in finding peace, joy and calmness in your life. Your family, friends and love is what really matters. Things that are of quality, not quantity!

The Dalai Lama, spiritual teacher and leader of Tibet, explains happiness this way… "I believe that the very purpose of life is to be happy. From the very core of our being, we desire contentment. In my own limited experience, I have found that the more we care for the happiness of others, the greater is our own sense of wellbeing. It is the principal source of success in life. Since we are not solely material creatures, it is a mistake to place all our hopes for happiness on external development alone. As human beings we all want to be happy and free from misery. We have learned that the key to happiness is inner peace. The greatest obstacles to inner peace are disturbing emotions such as anger, attachment, fear, and suspicion, while love, compassion, and a sense of universal responsibility, are the sources of peace and happiness."

WHAT THINGS CAN YOU DO TO BE HAPPIER TODAY?

1. _____.

2. _____.

3. _____.

4. _____.

5. _____.

"Success is getting what you want. Happiness is
wanting what you get."
—Dale Carnegie - Author of *How to Win Friends and Influence People*
(1888-1955)

COURSE SEVEN

Giving Forgiveness

Forgiveness sets the captive free.

You need to love and forgive yourself before you can love and forgive others. You can't give something to anyone that you don't already have. Forgiving unconditionally is one of the most challenging tests you'll ever take.

Unconditional means a total, wholehearted, complete, unrestricted, absolute, 100 percent letting go of all negative feelings and attachments to the wrongdoing and wrongdoer. It's a pardon, a reprieve, an amnesty, and an act of love, grace, and mercy.

> "We have all hurt someone tremendously, whether by intent or accident. But learning to forgive ourselves and others because we have not chosen wisely, is what makes us most human.
> We make horrible mistakes. It's how we learn.
> We breathe love. It's how we learn."
> — Nayyirah Waheed - Author of *Salt*

Forgiving yourself, for everything you regret doing and saying, will be one of the hardest things you will ever do for yourself. You can decide right now to love and forgive yourself and to learn from your past actions and reactions. When you choose to forgive yourself and others, you let go of the feelings of pain, frustration, conflict, anger, resentment, heartache, mental anguish, and everything that is keeping your already lived past in your present. You can't undo anything you've already done, but you can face up to it. You can tell the truth. You can seek forgiveness and then let love do the rest."

"Forgiveness is not a feeling; it is a commitment. It is a choice to show mercy, not to hold the offense up against the offender. Forgiveness is an expression of love."
— Dr. Gary Chapman – Author of *One More Try*

FORGIVE AGAIN AND LIVE AGAIN… When you pardon someone for his or her crime against you, you get all of the benefit because you are the one doing it. The healing, learning, changing, and growing are all used for your new and improved character. You cannot change the past or anyone else, so why would anyone in his right mind hold on to it? To forgive someone else's wrongdoing is to heal old wounds so you can regain your emotional health and wellbeing. You may or may not forget the act, yet you can remember it as a lesson learned so you won't allow it to happen again! Whether you are forgiving yourself or another person, the power and healing is always for you.

"To forgive someone is to set a prisoner free and to discover that the real prisoner was you!"
— Lewis B. Smedes - Author of *Forgive and Forget* (1921-2002)

Unforgiveness is wanting the past to be different and thinking you must hold onto it in your heart until it is! Forgiveness is the letting go of those feelings and making them different with each beat of your present heart. Forgiveness is an act of self-love that relieves and replaces those harmful feelings with joy, serenity, harmony, tranquility, and peace of mind. When we no longer hold a grudge against someone, it sets us free. When we are stuck in anger and unforgiveness too long, we end up leaving muddy footprints everywhere we go.

"When you hold resentment toward another, you are bound to that person or condition by an emotional link that is stronger than steel. Forgiveness is the only way to dissolve that link and get free."

— Catherine Ponder - Author of *The Prospering Power of Love*

Forgiving someone was never meant to be easy. It is easier said than done! It is always difficult, uncomfortable, and challenging. Forgiveness is never painless or trouble-free, yet unforgiveness always has enduring and harmful consequences. Bitterness and hatred is easy. It is always effortless and highly destructive. Hatred is a natural, emotional response to an unacceptable experience and can be passed from person to person, generation to generation.

Sometimes people say things they don't mean and do things they later wish they hadn't done. Words come out of our mouth that we can't take back, that hurt, wound, and inflict pain and suffering. Once you say something hurtful, you can't go back and fix it; what's done is done. Yet you can heal it, grow from it, and become a better person because of the laws of forgiveness.

"There is no love without forgiveness and there is no forgiveness without love."

— Bryant H. McGill - Author of *Voice of Reason*

127

When we forgive, we are dancing to the beat of God's loving heart. It is the tapping into the power of something greater than ourselves and much wiser than our emotions. Letting someone off the hook writes a new future in your emotional book of life. These are the life challenges that have the potential to produce more love and more life-changing empowerment, instead of more life-draining pain.

STOP BEATING YOURSELF UP... for your old mistakes. We all make mistakes and regret things in our pasts. Yet you're not your mistakes or your past. As the self-accused, you are the prosecution, defense attorney, and jury. Have mercy on yourself and don't judge yourself too much or too hard! You are here now with the power to shape your day and your future. Every single thing that has ever happened to you is preparing you for this very moment. Choose to use it all for good, for creating your best life today.

> "You have to say, 'I am forgiven' again and again, until it becomes the story you believe about yourself."
> — Cheryl Strayed - Author of *Tiny Beautiful Things*

• • • • • • •

I heard this inspiring story while I was driving and listening to talk radio... "A wise man sat in the audience and cracked a joke and everybody laughed like crazy. After a moment, he cracked the same joke again and this time less people laughed. He cracked the same joke again and again, and when there was no laughter in the crowd, he smiled and said, "You can't laugh at the same joke again and again, so why do you keep crying over the same thing over and over again?"

. . . .

Everyone has a past. It's all about what you learn from it, what you do with it and how you use it. The only place you can live is in the present and your past can either inspire you or poison you! No matter who you are, none of us get it right all of the time!

> "To err is human… to forgive is divine."
> —Alexander Pope - English Poet, "Essay on Man" (1688-1744)

Let's examine the root words of "Forgiveness"… "For" means in support of or to benefit. "Give" means to transfer freely the possession of something to someone. "Ness" denotes a state or condition. So, forgiveness is "The support for the decision to transfer an unwanted emotional possession into a new state of being." A powerful healing through receiving the benefits from giving, which changes your condition. No matter how dirty the dishes are, a little soap will always wash them clean.

> "To forgive is the highest, most beautiful form of love. In return, you will receive untold peace and happiness."
> —Robert Mueller - Author of *Fields Of War*

Forgiveness, gratitude, compassion, happiness, peace, joy, and kindness are all members of the "Loving Family." When you forgive others, you receive the family benefits of forgiveness. When you love others, you are given love in return, even when they don't love you back! When you're a friend to others, you will attract people who will be friendly to you. When you treat others kindly, they will treat you in the same way most of the time! Give and you will receive in ways you may not even realize. Work and you will receive your wages. Smile at the world and it will smile back at you! Laugh at life and happiness will be a part of your daily living experience.

Abraham Lincoln, self-educated lawyer, and sixteenth President of the United States, understood and lived the principles of forgiveness. He said… "Forgiveness is a secret that is hidden in plain sight. It costs nothing and is worth millions. It is available to everyone and used by few. If you harness the power of forgiveness, you will be sought after and highly regarded. And not coincidentally, you will also be forgiven by others." As President, he was criticized, rejected, mocked and assassinated for abolishing slavery. Yet he still chose to live an inspired life, emancipated by the proclamation of forgiveness.

Your emotional wounds can fester into infections if left untreated. That's exactly how blame works. Whatever was done to you gets under your skin, bruises your heart, and negatively effects your moods. Yet if you keep opening up the wound, exposing it to the germ-filled air, it will get infected and won't be able to heal. If the wound is not dressed and cleaned with the antiseptic of love and forgiveness, it will never heal. The wound will just fester until you become a sick, bitter, and unhappy person.

> "When a deep injury is done to us, we never recover until we forgive."
> —Alan Paton - Author of *Save The Beloved Country* (1903-1988)

We all have made some pretty big mistakes. Some of them seem to haunt us and the effects feel like they'll never go away. Like a medicine cures a disease, forgiveness washes away the symptoms of the emotional sickness that infects our emotions. Offering mercy heals the regret, remorse, and guilt that plague our ability to love ourselves and others. Love and forgiveness heal all wounds. They allow you to live a healthy and restored emotional life, with a positive state of mind. Love and forgiveness is the only way to stop your heart from bleeding.

"Never does the human soul appear so strong, as when it foregoes revenge and dares to forgive an injury."
— Edwin Hubbel Chapin – Poet, "Ocean Burial" (1814-1880)

UNFORGIVENESS… The "Un" part of "Unforgiveness" destroys us and creates negative emotions like Un-happy, Un-satisfied, Un-rest, Un-nerved, Un-healthy, and Un-comfortable… while too many times the other person doesn't even care or think about what he or she needs to be forgiven for! Meanwhile, you're carrying the guilt, misery, anger, and all of the related heavy burdens that go along with unforgiveness. People can become addicted to their suffering and relive it every time they tell their painful stories.

Della Reese, singer and TV personality from the hit show *Touched By An Angel* expresses it this way… "My idea of forgiveness is letting go of resentment that doesn't serve your better interest and ridding yourself of negative thoughts. All they do is make you miserable. Believe me, you can fret and fume all you want, but whoever it was that wronged you is not suffering from your anguish whatsoever."

In Tyler Perry's 2009 movie *Madea Goes To Jail*, there's a powerful scene where a street-hardened preacher talks about forgiveness. Having been a prostitute, she urges the prisoners to heed her advice and receive her wisdom that she had to learn the difficult way, on the streets! Sharing from her experiences, she compassionately tells the female inmates... "Forgiveness is not for the other person; it's for you. When you don't forgive somebody, you give them power over your life. They're sleeping at night and you're walking around remembering everything they've done. The longer you hold on to it, the longer you hold yourself back from being free."

HOLDING UNFORGIVENESS IN YOUR HEART... will give you an emotional heart attack! Your inability or choice not to get over what has happened in the past creates the resentment, bitterness, and unresolved anger that's like bad cholesterol to your emotional health. It's a blood clot that will clog your veins and stop the love from flowing into and out of your heart. Unforgiveness hurts us more than the person we need to forgive. Most of the time, the other person doesn't even care, whether you excuse his wrongdoing or not! He has already hardened his heart in order to handle his own guilt and regret. Unforgiveness is like drinking poison and expecting the other person to die!

I really enjoyed reading Andy Andrews' best-selling book *The Traveler's Gift*. After receiving so much inspiration, I just had to share a part of his forgiveness letter... "Now, the forgiveness that I hoarded has sprouted inside my heart, like a crippled seed yielding bitter fruit. No more! By the simple act of granting forgiveness, I release the demons of the past about which I can do nothing, and I create in myself a new heart, a new beginning."

The person who benefits most from forgiveness is the forgiver. Forgiveness sets you free from the damaged past and engages you in love's most challenging work, while receiving the physical, mental, emotional, spiritual, and financial benefits.

> "When you forgive, you in no way change the past,
> but you sure do change the future."
> — Bernard Meltzer - Radio Host, *What's Your Problem?* (1916-1998)

What they did is not acceptable, yet it is forgivable and forgettable. Feeling no resentment toward them is the medicine that restores you back to heart health. You will have to swallow your pride, do something you don't feel like doing, and go out of your way to forgive the person. Anything else is emotional and spiritual suicide! Unforgiveness is curable. Choose to become part of the solution for bringing peace to this earth, and let inner peace begin with me.

> "To be wronged is nothing, unless you continue to remember it."
> — Confucius - Chinese Teacher (551 BC-479 BC)

Every day, I am inspired by the words my Facebook friends post on my newsfeed. One of my friends, radio talk show host and writer, Hillary Raimo, posted this stirring message… "The greatest test of love is to love someone through their own hate, especially when it is directed at you! To be able to see them as beautiful pure beings of soul. To see their beauty even in their ugliness. To find them in spirit and meet them at their higher self. To go beyond the anger, the cut off, the harsh dark destructive place, that wishes to take your life and make you empty! Can you love me through my anger? Can I love you in yours? Can I hear you and understand what you are really saying?"

The only "Blame Game" you can win is when you take responsibility for your own life and hold yourself accountable with love, kindness and compassion. Then you must learn from your mistakes, while growing forward and upward. Forgiveness too often comes with a side order of blame. When you point your finger at someone else, more fingers are always pointing back at you.

> "Most of us can forgive and forget, we just don't want the
> other person to forget that we forgave."
> — Ivern Ball - Inspirational Online Writer

When we swing our sword of hatred, it cuts both ways! While we are hurting someone else, we are also hurting ourselves. So before you embark on a journey of revenge and getting even, go out and dig two graves. Resentment, unforgiveness, and anger kill more people than bullets do! They are spiritual, physical, and emotional cancers that destroy people from the inside out, ruining their emotional health. "Burying the hatchet" breaks the negative feelings that connect you to the harmful event and destructive past.

Too many people just want to forget, without turning it into something learned. Absolution is not forgetting the past, but healing the present. It is not about excusing the wrongdoing;

it's about correcting it by releasing it from your heart. Through giving a reprieve to the ones who hurt you, you're preventing the unpleasant past from affecting your present in a bad way. Forgiving breaks the harmful cycle of pain, resentment, suffering, guilt, blame, irritation, and punishment.

Henry Ward Beecher, social reformer and abolitionist, said it so powerfully when he wrote… "I can forgive, but I cannot forget, is only another way of saying, I will not forgive. Forgiveness should be like a cancelled note torn in two and burned up, so it never can be shown against anyone. Sometimes you just have to forgive what you can't forget and forget what you can't forgive."

IN ORDER TO LOVE YOUR ENEMIES… and forgive those who have hurt you, you must go to war with yourself and fight against everything you think and feel. Change your thinking, forgive your enemy, and you'll change your hurting world. Oscar Wilde, nineteenth century author and playwright, said this after spending two unjustified years in prison… "Always forgive your enemies, nothing annoys them so much."

WE CAN'T MAKE ANYONE FORGIVE OR LOVE US… You can only offer it or ask for it from others. The results are out of your control. Turning a blind eye to what has been done to you in the past creates the greatest insight into your emotional healing. When you give love and forgiveness with no expectations of getting anything in return, you are set free from the results. You are now empowered by the act of kindness and compassion. You no longer own the unforgiveness and choose to live without the negative effects. You can only do this in love and the lightness of your spirit.

"Sincere forgiveness isn't colored with expectations that the other person apologizes or changes. Love them and release them. Life feeds back truth to people in its own way and time."
— Sarah Maddison - Author of *Beyond White Guilt*

BECOME A HAPPIER AND HEALTHIER PERSON... by practicing forgiveness. Friedrich Nietzsche, nineteenth century philosopher and poet, inspired others by saying, "If your friend does evil to you, say to him, "I forgive you for what you did to me, but how can I forgive you for what you did to yourself?" Ann Landers, in her famous "Ask Ann Landers" syndicated advice column, wrote, "One of the secrets of a long and fruitful life is to forgive everybody everything, before you go to bed."

Many times, people have gone to my website inlifeschool.com to seek my life coaching advice on a personal challenge they're experiencing. I'm deeply moved by their asking for my help and always have the best intentions within my heartfelt response. Here is just one example of what I receive in my inbox…

· · · · · · ·

FACEBOOK MESSAGE SENT: Dear Rob…

"How do I forgive myself for leaving my husband for a new life with another man? Today, I am back with my husband although we are divorced. We have been together for 25 years, however I'm beating myself up and today is a particularly bad day! I am a kind and loving person and I just don't like myself for what I did, even though there were reasons to justify my leaving. We had problems and I never gave it a second chance, because I had fallen in love. The other man never loved me and within two weeks he had found a "new love." I know I love my ex-husband for sure, but I'm killing myself with self-loathing and guilt. Basically, I'm reaching out for some words of wisdom. As I type to you, I am lying in a darkened room battling to face it all. Generally I am a cheerful soul, but this is hard."

MY FACEBOOK REPLY BACK TO HER…

"Just remember, no amount of beating yourself up will ever make you or the people around you feel good. Loving and forgiving yourself is something only you can do. Talk to your husband about it. Ask for his forgiveness and accept it for both of your healing. There is something there that needs to be dealt with, that is why it's surfacing in guilt. I hope this helps… Love and peace."

HER FACEBOOK RESPONSE BACK TO ME…

"Thank you so much. All you say is very deeply felt. I just had a discussion with my husband and brought some issues in the open. Love and light."

MY LAST FACEBOOK REPLY BACK TO HER…

"The truth will always set you free from your self-imposed prison! The healing process may be uncomfortable, but the unhealed emotions are causing you way more discomfort. The pain will bring you and your husband closer, as long as you face it, experience it, and heal it together."

• • • • • • •

"The message should not be to forgive one another, rather understand one another."
— Emma Goldman - Political Activist (1869-1940)

Martin Luther King, on his mission for equal rights preached, "He who is devoid of the power to forgive, is devoid of the power to love."

Mahatma Gandhi, in his quest for freedom, said, "The weak can never forgive. Forgiveness is the attribute of the strong."

Jesus said, "Let all bitterness, wrath, anger, complaints, and slander be put away from you, releasing all evil intentions. Be kind to one another, tenderhearted, forgiving each other. Put on, therefore, a heart of compassion, kindness, humility, and perseverance. Above all these things, walk in love, which is the bond of perfection. Don't let the sun go down on your anger. Love your enemies and bless those who mistreat you. He who has been forgiven much, loves much."

Buddha said, "To understand everything is to forgive everything."

Mark Twain, author of *The Adventures of Tom Sawyer*, put it like this… "The ability to forgive is the true test of greatness. It teaches us the art of living and loving. Our own weakness and flaws make us sympathetic towards other people's mistakes. We will be forgiven to the degree that we forgive others. To mess up is human, to forgive is divine. Forgiving and forgetting is the best revenge. Forgiveness is the fragrance the flower sheds on the heel that crushed it."

· · · · · · ·

A CALL FOR ACTION

Your Forgiveness List

A simple and powerful way to start the emotional healing process is to make a "Forgiveness List." Invest some time into taking steps toward forgiving yourself and others by filling out this list. Do this for yourself first and you'll feel better, think better, look better, love better, live better, and be a happier person for doing it.

SO LET'S GET STARTED...

What things do I need to forgive myself for?

1. _____.

2. _____.

3. _____.

4. _____.

5. _____.

What do I need to forgive others for, whether they deserve it or not?

1. _____.

2. _____.

3. _____.

4. _____.

5. _____.

"Forgive and forget. Many say, 'Yes, I do forgive, but I will never forget.' Beware of this sentiment, for it leaves you subtly in the thrall of suffering. Do forget what was done to you, just remember the lessons you learned from it. Drop the cross. Embrace the sky."

— Marianne Williamson - Author of *A Return to Love*

Who needs to forgive me, by my asking them for their forgiveness?

1. _____.

2. _____.

3. _____.

4. _____.

5. _____.

What else is in your heart that needs forgiving?

_____

_____

_____

_____

_____

"When I am able to resist the temptation to judge others, I can see them as teachers of forgiveness in my life, reminding me that I can only have peace of mind when I forgive rather than judge."

— Jerry Jampolsky – Author of *Forgiveness: The Greatest Healer of All*

COURSE EIGHT

Living In Gratitude

You can buy a $100,000 luxury car, yet it is worthless without a $4 gallon of gas. Gratitude is the fuel that transports love, peace, joy, happiness, health, and positive attitude through your life. Gratitude is a luxury we can all afford because it costs so little to be it and benefit from it.

Gratitude is the attitude and feeling of being thankful. It is the returning of kindness given, the sincere expression of appreciation. It's something you must practice; it doesn't automatically happen. You become full of gratitude by going through your day, finding things to be grateful for. It's an act of acknowledgment, that is the key to all things spiritual, emotional, material, and financial.

"Count your blessings. Once you realize how valuable you are and how much you have going for you, the smiles will return, the sun will break out, the music will play, and you will finally be able to move forward into the life that God intended for you with grace, strength, courage, and confidence."

— Og Mandino - Author of *The Choice* (1923-1996)

Pause during your busy day and take a few moments to reflect on what is good in your life, no matter how large or small those things may be. Take the time to thank life for all it has given you, and others for the treasured things they have contributed. You already have so many amazing things in your life to be grateful for, whether you realize it or not! Gratitude, with an optimistic attitude for what you have, opens the doors to getting what you want and completes the cycle of getting what you need. So if you want and need more, then increase your feelings of being thankful for everything you already have.

· · · · · · ·

A VERY GRATEFUL PERSPECTIVE

Be thankful that you don't already have everything you desire. If you did, what would there be to look forward to?

Be thankful when you don't know something,
for it gives you the opportunity to learn.

Be thankful for the difficult times,
for during these times you grow.

Be thankful for your limitations,
because they give you opportunities for improvement.

Be thankful for each new challenge,
because it will build your strength and character.

Be thankful for your mistakes,
they will teach you valuable lessons.

Be thankful when you're tired and weary,
because it means you've made a difference.

· · · · · · ·

It's easy to be thankful for the good things. A life of rich fulfillment comes to those who are also thankful for the setbacks. Gratitude can turn a negative into a positive. Find a way to be thankful for your troubles and they can become your greatest blessings.

A POSITIVE ATTITUDE CREATES GRATITUDE... and enables you to make the best of every situation. It gives you power over your circumstances, instead of allowing your circumstances to have power over you. Even when you perceive that, "The grass is greener on the other side of your street," you're still going to have to mow the lawn and pull the weeds on that side too! An inspired attitude of gratitude changes the way you look at all things.

"He who is richest, is grateful and content with the least."
— Socrates - Greek Philosopher (469 BC-399 BC)

· · · · · · ·

LIFE IS A GIFT... So today before you say an unkind word, think of someone who can't speak or is suffering from verbal abuse.

Before you complain about the taste of your food, think of someone who has nothing to eat and no clean water to drink.

Before you complain about your husband or wife, think of someone who's crying out for a companion or has just gone through a divorce.

Before you complain about life, think of someone who died far too early or has only a short time to live.

Before you complain about your children, think of someone who wants children but is barren or whose child is missing.

Before you argue about your dirty house that someone didn't clean, think of the people who are living in the streets or have lost their homes in storms or due to bankruptcy.

And when you are tired and complain about your job, think of the unemployed, the disabled, and those who wish they had your job.

And before you think of pointing the finger or condemning another, remember that not one of us is without wrong.

And when depressing thoughts seem to get you down, choose to put a smile on your face and be thank that you're alive!

Life is a gift... Live it... Enjoy it... Celebrate it... Love it...

Are you grateful yet?

• • • • • • •

TRY TO BE GRATEFUL... for the difficult and challenging situations that arise in your life. It is often through these circumstances that we experience the most profound spiritual and emotional growth. You can learn to view each perceived obstacle as an opportunity to develop a new quality, strength, skill, or insight, and to be grateful for the lessons your life experiences are giving you.

144

"Gratitude is not only the greatest of virtues,
but the parent of all the others."
— Marcus Tullius Cicero - Roman Statesman (106 BC-43 BC)

It's easy to be thankful for the good things that you already have that bring health, success, happiness, and fulfillment. For those who are looking for the deeper meaning and higher purpose in living, gratitude comes to those who are also thankful for their set-backs and losses.

For it's when you are in the valleys of your life that you look up and see the highest mountaintop. It's when you have climbed out of the low land and onto the tallest peak, that you become filled with the awe-inspiring gratitude for being blessed with the strength to have risen above your situation.

Gratitude turns a negative feeling into a positive thought, and an unpleasant experience into a valuable lesson. When you find a way to be thankful for your troubles, they will become your greatest blessings and sources of inspiration. The fruits of gratitude are love, peace, joy, happiness, and goodness… just to pick a few.

Melody Beattie, in her book *Make Miracles In Forty Days: Turning What You Have Into What You Want*, explains gratitude like this… "Gratitude unlocks the fullness of life. It turns what we have into enough, and more. It can turn a meal into a feast, a house into a home, a stranger into a friend. Gratitude makes sense of our past, brings peace for today and creates a vision for tomorrow."

· · · · · · ·

AN INTERVIEW WITH GOD

I dreamed I had an interview with God... "Come in," God said. "So, you would like to interview Me?" "If you have the time," I replied. God smiled and said, "My time is eternity. It is enough to do everything. What questions do you have in mind to ask me?"

I asked, "What surprises you most about mankind?" God thought for a few moments and then answered, "That they lose their health to make money and then lose their money to restore their health. That by thinking anxiously about the future, they live neither for the present nor the future. That they live as if they will never die, and die as if they had never lived."

God placed my hands in His and we were silent for while. Then I asked, "As a parent, what are some of life's lessons you want your children to learn?" God replied with a smile, "To learn that they cannot make anyone love them. What they can do is to let themselves be loved. To learn that what is most valuable isn't what they have in their lives, but whom they have in their lives. To learn that it's not good to compare themselves to others. All will be judged individually on their own merits, not as a group on a comparison basis. And also to learn that a rich person isn't the one who has the most, but the one who needs the least. To learn that it only takes a few seconds to open profound wounds in people we love, and it takes many years to heal them. To learn to forgive by practicing forgiveness. To learn that there are people who love them dearly, but simply do not know how to express or show their feelings. To learn that money can buy everything but happiness. To learn that two people can look at the same thing and see it totally differently. To learn that a true friend is someone who knows everything about them and likes them anyway. To learn that it isn't always enough that they be forgiven by others, but that they have to forgive themselves."

I sat there for a while enjoying my visit with God. I thanked Him for His time and for all He has done for my family and me. He replied, "Anytime. I'm here twenty-four hours a day. All you have to do is ask for Me, and I'll answer your call."

• • • • • • •

FOCUS ON… your successes, not your failures.

FOCUS ON… the things you have, not what you don't have.

FOCUS ON… who you are and not who you used to be.

FOCUS ON… what you are doing now, not what you didn't do.

FOCUS ON… what you are learning, not on what you don't know.

FOCUS ON… your good habits and not the bad ones.

FOCUS ON… the positive, not the negative things in life.

FOCUS ON… your strengths, not your weaknesses.

FOCUS ON… the love in your life and not the fear.

• • • • • • •

Seeds of discouragement, depression, and hopelessness cannot take root in a grateful and loving heart. Be grateful for the small things, for they add up to become the big things you have to be thankful for. Awaken to the joy, peace, love, and happiness within your ordinary moments.

Rhonda Byrne, author of *The Secret*, advises us to "Be grateful for what you have now. As you begin to think about all the things in your life you are grateful for, you will be amazed at the never-ending thoughts that come back to you of more things to be grateful for."

REASONS FOR BEING THANKFUL… If you woke up this morning with more health than illness, you are more blessed than the millions who won't survive this week. Twenty-six hundred Americans woke up yesterday expecting to live for a long time and today they passed away.

If you have money in the bank, in your wallet, and spare change in a dish someplace, you are among the top 8 percent of the world's wealthy. In 2012, the U.S. Census Bureau reported that nearly 50 million Americans or over 16 percent of the U.S. population live below the poverty line.

If you have never experienced the danger of battle, the loneliness of imprisonment, the agony of torture, the pains of slavery, or the pangs of starvation, you are ahead of 500 million people in the world who have. If you can read this information, you are more fortunate than the approximately two billion people in the world who can't read.

If you have food in the refrigerator, clothes on your back, a roof over your head and a place to sleep, you are richer than 75 percent of the people living in today's world.

WITH ENOUGH FOOD GROWN ON THIS PLANET... to feed its people three times over, what a wake-up call I had when I read these eye-opening, heart-wrenching, world hunger statistics. This isn't easy to think about, look at, or pleasant to read, yet it should make you feel very grateful for all you have. It surely gave me a renewed attitude of gratitude.

Approximately 35,615 people a day die of starvation worldwide. That's over one million people a month and over 15 million men, women, and children a year. Somewhere around 85 percent of these starvation deaths occur in children five years of age or younger, with around 16,438 children dying every day. Every three seconds, another one of our fellow human beings dies from lack of food and healthy water.

"Be thankful for what you have and you'll end up having more. If you concentrate on what you don't have, you will never, ever have enough. Gratitude is the single greatest thing you can use to change your life."
— Oprah Winfrey - TV Personality, Philanthropist

· · · · · · ·

FORGIVE ME WHEN I WHINE

Today upon a bus, I saw a girl with golden hair. I envied her, she seemed so happy, and I wished I was as fair. When suddenly she rose to leave, I saw her hobble down the aisle. She had one leg and used a crutch, but as she passed, she gave me a smile. Oh God, forgive me when I whine. I have two legs, the world is mine.

I stopped to buy some candy, the lad who sold it had such charm. I talked with him, he seemed so glad, if I were late, it'd do no harm. And as I left, he said to me, "I thank you, you've been so kind." It's nice to talk with folks like you, you see, he said, "I am blind." Oh God, forgive me when I whine. I have two eyes, the world is mine.

Later while walking down the street, I saw a child with eyes of blue. He stood and watched the others play, he seemed to not know what to do. I stopped a moment and then I said, "Why don't you join the others dear?" He looked ahead without a word, and then I knew he couldn't hear. Oh God, forgive me when I whine. I have two ears, the world is mine.

With feet to take me where I'd go, with eyes to see the sunset's glow, With ears to hear what I would know, Oh God, forgive me when I whine. I've been blessed indeed, the world is mine.

· · · · · · ·

A GRATITUDE PROCESS… Close your eyes for one minute and think of yourself as being blind. Then open up your eyes and give thanks for the gift of sight. Lie down on the floor and imagine yourself not being able to get up. Then rise and be thankful for your legs and arms. Hold your hands over your ears and imagine yourself being deaf. Then take your hands away and give thanks for the gift of hearing. Open your mouth and speak silence with your lips. Then sing and shout thanks that you can talk. This simple process produces a whole bunch of gratitude and a renewed thankful attitude for the gifts you have been given.

. . . .

THE SEVEN WONDERS OF THE WORLD

1. To see

2. To hear

3. To touch

4. To taste

5. To feel

6. To laugh

7. To love

. . . .

We all need to be reminded of the precious and priceless gifts we have and what we can be grateful for. Being grateful for the little things, will have a big effect on our level of happiness, love, peace, and joy.

"Too many people get caught up in the noise of everyday life to truly hear the symphony of what life is really all about."
— Robert Werner - Inspirational Writer

. . . .

One day while I was golfing... I pinched a nerve in my neck. The next day I woke up with a completely numb right hand. When I rose from my bed, being right-handed, I soon found out that I couldn't hold toilet paper, a toothbrush, or a glass of water. Ordinary things like putting on my clothes, shaving, making breakfast and typing on the computer were all a challenge. When I went to work, putting the house key in the lock and starting my car was very difficult.

I was totally freaked out! I began to panic and fill with anxiety as I thought about what my life would be like if I didn't regain the normal use of my hand. All of the simple things I never thought about being grateful for were quickly getting my attention!

I could only use my left hand and I was hoping and praying that the chiropractor could help me. After many months of therapy, most of the feeling returned and the use of my right hand is close to normal. Wow, what a relief. I will never take the use of my hands for granted again.

· · · · · · ·

If you want to feel wealthy, then count up all the priceless things you have that money can't buy, and you will think and grow rich. Begin to stop complaining about the aches and pains you do have and switch your thoughts to being grateful for the "aches and pains" you don't have!

As Joni Mitchell wrote and sang, "Don't it always seem to go, that you don't know what you've got till it's gone." We don't have to wait until things are gone before we appreciate what we have. Love, laughter, freedom, and health, brings to you the kind of wealth, that's worth more than the cost, of getting them back after they are lost.

· · · · · · ·

Just imagine... waking up tomorrow morning and being too sick to get out of bed. In fact, you're so sick, you may never be able to take care of yourself, go to work again, run or play, or go for a walk on a sunny day! How would things look different to you then?

You're now deeply longing for the ability to feed and clean yourself, to breathe without pain, and to live without feeling sick. You passionately miss the wind in your face, the sun on your back, the smell of fresh air, the awesome sight of the stars, and the simple pleasure of a scenic drive.

If you could just get your life back to the way things were, when you were always complaining about things and had an ungrateful attitude about life.

If you could, you would promise to be thankful for the simple things you never realized were so valuable. You would seldom whine about people, places, and things, problems, working too hard, driving in bad traffic, doing yard work, having to do the dishes, taking out the garbage or having to do what you don't feel like doing. Your attitude of gratitude level would go sky high and your complaining spirit would go far, far away.

You would consider yourself a complete success in life, if you could take a shower, go to the bathroom on your own, walk out the door, use a fork, and bring home a paycheck. Your focus would be on what you have, instead of what you don't have. You would now see your cup as half-full, instead of half-empty. Your thoughts and feelings would be filled with what you are now doing, instead of what you could, would, or should have done.

Regretting and blaming would be something you would hardly do, without being painfully aware of how it robs you of your joy. You would be full of thanksgiving for all of the things you used to take for granted, before your illness took them away from you! You would have learned the lesson that in order to live a healthy and successful life, you must be grateful for and love your life, no matter what!

· · · · · · ·

Leo Buscaglia, author of *Born for Love*, writes about his Buddhist teacher in Thailand who would remind his students that there was always something to be thankful for. His teacher would say, "Let's rise and be thankful, for if we didn't learn a lot today, at least we may have learned a little. And if we didn't learn even a little, at least we didn't get sick. And if we did get sick, at least we didn't die. So let us all be thankful."

· · · · · · ·

THE MASTER'S LESSON ON GRATITUDE

According to legend, a young man while roaming the desert came across a spring of delicious crystal clear water. The water was so sweet, he filled his leather canteen so he could bring some back to a tribal elder, who had been his teacher.

After a four-day journey he presented the water to the old man who took a deep drink, smiled warmly, and thanked his student lavishly for the sweet water. The young man returned to his village with a happy heart. Later, the teacher let another student taste the water. He spat it out, saying it was awful. It apparently had become stale because of the old leather container.

The student challenged his teacher, "Master, the water was foul. Why did you pretend to like it?" The teacher replied, "You only tasted the water. I tasted the gift. The water was simply the container for an act of love and kindness and nothing could be sweeter!"

· · · · · · ·

Grateful people love themselves and others more, and are happier in most things. They are more positive and optimistic and they cope with life better. Thankful people handle negative situations more easily, have good people skills, and choose to grow and learn from their experiences. They sleep better, are healthier, and have a better attitude. As a character trait, gratitude is one of the strongest links to good mental health. Gratitude is the key to a long, prosperous, and enjoyable life. Love and gratitude are the spices which bring out the desirable flavors in life.

"If a person isn't thankful for what they've got, they aren't
likely to be thankful for what they're going to get."
— Frank A. Clark - Spiritual Cartoonist (1911-1991)

Too many of us wait until Valentine's Day to show our love
for others, Christmas to give gifts to people we value, Mother's
Day and Father's Day to express our appreciation for our par-
ents, and Thanksgiving to be grateful for everything we have.
Gratitude and appreciation feeds our hunger and quenches our
thirst for more. Everyone takes, not everyone gives thanks.

"Gratitude helps you to grow and expand. Gratitude brings
joy and laughter into your life and into the lives
of all those around you."
— Eileen Caddy - The Findhorn Foundation (1917-2006)

LIFE TALKS TO US IN MANY WAYS… When you get news
of a sick friend, life is telling you to be grateful for your health
and to take care of yourself. When you turn on the nightly news
and see all of the pain and suffering in the world, the universe
is saying to be grateful for all you have. When you hear about
someone having an accident, tell yourself how thankful you are
for being safe today. When you hear about someone getting
married or someone expresses how happy he or she is, acknowledge all of the love and happiness in your life that you may or
may not be feeling. When you get the news of a loved one who
has passed away, realize that life is just a vapor, gratitude is the
key to happiness, and you are so blessed to still be alive!

"Develop an attitude of gratitude, and give thanks for
everything that happens to you, knowing that every step
forward is a step toward achieving something bigger
and better than your current situation."
— Brian Tracy - Author of *Change Your Thinking, Change Your Life*

· · · · · · ·

RICH DAD, WISER SON

One day, the father of a very wealthy family took his son on a trip to the country with the express purpose of showing him how poor people live. They spent a couple of days and nights on the farm of what would be considered a very poor family.

While returning home from their trip, the father asked his son, "How was the trip?" It was great, Dad, the son replied. "Did you see how poor people live?" the father asked. "Oh yeah," said the son. "So tell me, what did you learn from the trip?" asked the father.

The son answered, "I saw that we have one dog and they had four. We have a pool that reaches to the middle of our garden and they have a creek that has no end. We have imported lanterns in our garden and they have the stars at night. Our patio reaches to the front yard and they have the whole horizon. We have a small piece of land to live on and they have fields that go beyond our sight. We have servants who serve us, but they serve others. We buy our food, but they grow theirs. We have walls around our property to protect us, they have friends to protect them." The boy's father was speechless. Then his son added, "Thanks, Dad, for showing me how poor we are!"

· · · · · · ·

LIFE IS ALL ABOUT HOW YOU CHOOSE TO SEE IT. CHANGE YOUR THINKING, CHANGE YOUR WORLD.

Expressing gratitude on a daily basis is a very positive and fulfilling exercise to practice, and a great way to renew a thankful spirit in your heart, mind, and soul. When you go to bed at night and lay your head upon your pillow, what thoughts run through your mind as you fall asleep? When the alarm goes off and you open up your eyes to a new day, what do you think about?

"Just now, the sun and my gratitude arose in the same breath."
— Aleya Hart - Inspirational Online Writer

Counting your blessings will focus your energy on what you have and your thoughts will continue to add to your list throughout your day. When you get into bed at night, make a mental list of at least five things you can be grateful for. Falling asleep with gratitude in your heart and mind will improve your dreams, the quality of your rest, and your overall wellbeing. Cultivating the habit of counting your blessings will plant the seeds of gratitude, which will reap a harvest of health, love, and happiness.

Each day before your feet hit the floor in the morning, lie in bed and create a mental list of at least five things you are grateful for. You might give thanks for a new day of fresh opportunities, food, love, health, shelter, friends, family, your job, the air you breathe and your beating heart. The "Law of Attraction" says that like attracts like and the more you live in gratitude, the more things you will be given to be grateful for.

Scientific studies show you're happier when you exercise gratitude upon waking and going to sleep. You become more optimistic, healthier, achieve more of your goals, and are more loving and giving throughout your day. When you invest some effort, contemplation, recognition, and meditation, you'll have both immediate and long-term positive effects in your life.

Counting your blessings is the easiest math to learn, once you see how your life adds up to so much more, when you acknowledge the things you have to be grateful for. Thankfulness unlocks the abundance of life by turning what we have into enough and so much more. It has the power to turn a humble meal into a feast, a glass of water into fine wine, or a house into a palace.

I AM THANKFUL BECAUSE… I can see, hear, smell, talk, walk, taste, think, and feel. I am so grateful for my health, the roof over my head, water in my faucet, food in the refrigerator, a car that works, money in the bank, a computer, books, a good job, beautiful music, and an abundance of things stored in boxes.

I AM BLESSED… because I have a cell phone, a guitar, vitamins, a toothbrush, clothes, soap, electricity, the Internet, a toilet, a shower, a TV, air conditioning, a surfboard, furniture, shoes, and most of everything I need.

· · · · · · ·

A CALL FOR ACTION

Your Gratitude List

Gratitude takes practice. You must take part in it every day. Research shows that when people put into words what they feel grateful for, they have a much richer and greater life experience.

Studies prove that people who exercise the act of being grateful, have a stronger sense of wellbeing, are less depressed, less stressed, more generous, more forgiving, have better relationships, and ex-perience an overall higher level of satisfaction in life.

Everyone has at least five things to be grateful for every day. You need to be grateful now, not tomorrow or when you get this or do that. When you plant the seeds of joy, love, peace, and happiness in the soil of "thankfulness," your life will thrive and prosper!

MAKE FILLING OUT THIS GRATITUDE LIST A DAILY PRACTICE. Then keep what you have written in a "Gratitude Journal," so you can go back and read it months later.

Take a moment to reflect on what you are grateful for. Then plant them in the fields below...

I am grateful for _____.

I am grateful for _____.

I am grateful for _____.

I am grateful for _____.

I am grateful for _____.

"Feeling gratitude and not expressing it,
is like wrapping a present and not giving it."
— William Arthur Ward - Author of *Fountains of Faith* (1921-1994)

I appreciate _____.

I appreciate _____.

I appreciate _____.

I appreciate _____.

I appreciate _____.

"Cultivate the habit of being grateful for every good thing that
comes to you, and to give thanks continuously."
— Ralph Waldo Emerson - Poet, "The Snow-Storm" (1803-1882)

I am thankful for _____.

I am thankful for _____.

I am thankful for _____.

I am thankful for _____.

I am thankful for _____.

"Thank You is the best prayer that anyone could say. Thank you
expresses extreme gratitude, humility, and understanding."
— Alice Walker - Author of *The Color Purple*

COURSE NINE

Experience Is Your Teacher

We are all students and experience is our greatest teacher. Not everyone goes to college, yet we all attend "Life School." In this school of life, we're given the exam first, and only after we've gone through the test are we given the lesson. Don't just go through life; grow and evolve through life! Knowledge is information. Wisdom is applying the knowledge toward living a more successful and fulfilling life.

> "Experience isn't what happens to you. It's what you
> do with what happens to you."
> — Aldous Huxley - Author of *Brave New World* (1894-1963)

When we were in high school, we would learn a subject in class, study for and take a test, and then after it was graded, the teacher would go over the exam and give us the right answers. They did this so we would learn from our mistakes and become a smarter, better, and wiser person. Life is exactly like that. We get it wrong, so we can learn how to do it right. Be wise, don't regret it... get it!

> "I was always willing to acknowledge my own self, as the
> principal cause of every good and evil which may happen to
> me. Therefore I have always found myself capable of being
> my own pupil, and ready to love my teacher."
> — Giacomo Casanova - Famous Lover (1725-1798)

Learning from your experiences is the natural way of teaching yourself what you need to know. Having to repeat the lessons your life wants to teach you is the result of not learning the lessons the first time around. Yet it's okay and normal not to get it right the first, second, or even the third time! It is like memorizing something. You have to repeat it over and over again, until you have it etched into your memory.

"Your journey has molded you for your greater good and it was exactly what it needed to be. Don't think that you've lost time. There is no shortcutting to life. It took each and every situation you have encountered, to bring you to the now.
And now is right on time."
—Asha Tyson - Author of *How I Retired At 26*

Life will continue to present you with the opportunity to learn the lesson until you have achieved it. Then you are given another test and another lesson to learn, then another test, another lesson and so on and so on...

"By three methods we may learn wisdom. First, by reflection which is the noblest. Second, by imitation which is the easiest. And third by experience, which is the most bitter."
—Confucius - Chinese Philosopher (551 BC-479 BC)

The New Oxford American Dictionary defines "experience" as the knowledge or skill acquired through an incident, happening, adventure, or encounter. An occurrence that leaves an impression on someone. To go through, participation in, exposure to, awareness of, and insight into. Experience is skill, practical knowledge, understanding, maturity, and informal know-how.

"I have come to the frightening conclusion, that I am the decisive element in all things that I experience in life. I possess tremendous power to make life miserable or joyous. I can be an instrument of inspiration. I can hurt or heal. In all situations, it is my response that decides whether a crisis is escalated or de-escalated, and a person is humanized or de-humanized."
— Goethe - German Writer (1749-1832)

Experience is often referred to as "The School of Hard-Knocks," and said to be the best teacher. Yet the tuition is sometimes very, very high! It isn't always the kindest of teachers, but it always turns out to be the best kind. The problems, victories, difficulties, successes, and all of the things in your life bring experience and experience brings wisdom.

"Every experience you are having is bringing you closer to your true self."
— Panache Desai - Author of *Discovering Your Soul Signature*

• • • • • • •

JUST BE

When life is not as amazing as you want it to be,
When love is not as passionate as it used to be,
When happiness is not as present as it could be,
When things are not as fun as they should be,
Take a moment, look up and see,
We are all born to learn... how to just be.

• • • • • • •

165

Gary Zukav writes in his wisdom filled book *The Seat of the Soul*... "When the personality comes fully to serve the energy of its soul, that is authentic empowerment. Every experience that you have and will have upon the earth, encourages the alignment of the personality with your soul."

We were all born to make mistakes and learn from them. Wrong decisions, bad choices, negative thinking, complaining, a poor attitude, and all of the other unpleasant personal experiences are all a part of the process of learning how to live a better and best life today. Our personal power is in controlling the mental, emotional, physical, and spiritual effects it has on us!

"In the business world, everyone is paid in two coins: Cash and Experience. Take the experience first; the cash will come later."
— Harold Geneen - Author of *Managing* (1910-1997)

When you choose to feel disappointed about things not being the way you hoped and expected they could, would, and should have turned out, you rob yourself of the positive energy you need to transform your what, where, and how, into your good, better, and best life now!

"There is only one thing more painful than learning from experience and that is, not learning from experience."
—Archibald MacLeish - Poet, "Conquistador" (1892-1982)

All of us have bad and unfair things happen to us; it's just a part of life. We all will go through trials and tribulations, gains and losses, happiness and depression. The key is to be grateful in the good times and the problem times, while believing you will be better, stronger, and more prosperous than before your challenges began. It's your own free will that chooses whether to be bitter or better off as a result of your experiences.

"Carefully watch your thoughts, for they become your words. Manage and choose your words, for they will become your actions. Consider and judge your actions, for they become your habits. Acknowledge and watch your habits, for they shall become your values. Understand and embrace your values, for they become your destiny."
— Mahatma Gandhi - Philosopher (1869-1948)

When you are facing a challenge or problem, don't look for a way around it or out of it; look for the way through it. Life is in the lesson. It sometimes takes you into troubled waters, not to drown you, but to cleanse you. We go through things so we can change and grow through things.

"There are no failures, just experiences
and your reactions to them."
— Tom Krause - Opera Singer (1934-2013)

Life is so ironic. It takes sadness to know what happiness is, noise to appreciate silence, and absence to value presence. There is no pleasure without some pain, no good without a little bad, and no success without some failures. It is simply the way of the world we live and breathe in. The one thing we can control is how we go up and down the ladders of life and whether they take us to a lower or higher place. Step by step, we are all climbing our stairway to heaven.

"Life will give you whatever experience is most helpful for the evolution of your consciousness. How do you know this is the experience you need? Because this is the experience you are having at the moment. The primary cause of unhappiness is never the situation, but your thoughts about it."
— Eckhart Tolle - Author of *A New Earth*

· · · · · · ·

I prayed for strength… and life gave me difficulties to make me strong.

I asked for wisdom… and life gave me problems to solve.

I hoped for prosperity… and life gave me brain and brawn to work.

I prayed for courage… and life gave me dangers to overcome.

I asked for love… and life gave me troubled people to help.

I hoped for favors… and life gave me opportunities.

· · · · · · ·

"Every happening great or small is a parable by which God speaks to us, and the art of life is to get the message!"
— Malcolm Muggeridge - Author of *Something Beautiful for God* (1903-1990)

I really enjoyed reading Cherie Carter-Scott's inspirational book, *If Life Is A Game, These Are The Rules*. Here are two of her rules that reflect and help strengthen the ideas written throughout this book…

1. Growth is a process of experimentation, a series of trials, errors and occasional victories. The failed experiments are as much a part of the process as the experiments that work.

2. There is no part of life that does not contain its lessons. If you are alive, there are lessons to be learned.

> "I don't care how smart a kid you are. The only way you learn what's not right is from experience."
> — Cameron Diaz - Actress, Author of *The Body Book*

. . . .

I Want To Thank… those who hated me, you made me love myself more.

Thanks to those who loved me, you made my heart grow stronger.

Thanks to those who cared, you made me feel so special.

Thanks to those who came into my life, you helped me become who I am today.

Thanks to those who went away, you showed me that nothing lasts forever.

Thanks to those who stuck by me, you showed me what real friendship is all about.

Thanks to those who listened, you made me feel like I was worth your time.

. . . .

"Every single thing you've been through, every single moment that you've come through, were all to prepare you for this moment right now. Now you get that you are the creator of your destiny. No one else can dance your dance, sing your song or write your story."
— Lisa Nichols - Author of *No Matter What!*

Life is what you decide to make it. No regrets, mistakes, or failures, only lessons. You have the miraculous power to look back on everything you did yesterday and change what didn't work and empower what did! You had to go down that road to get where you are now. You had to go through it in order to learn from it! As you sail through life and voyage upon unknown seas, don't avoid the rougher waters. Because calm waters and a smooth voyage won't help you become a better sailor.

"This very moment is the perfect teacher, and lucky for us, it's with us wherever we are."
— Pema Chodron - Author of *When Things Fall Apart*

· · · · · · · ·

MAY LIFE GIVE YOU

Enough trials to make you stronger.
Enough sorrow to keep you grateful.
Enough happiness to keep away heartache.
Enough hope to make you ambitious.
Enough failure to keep you successful.
Enough enthusiasm to make you motivated.
Enough friends to keep you company.

Enough wealth to make life easier.

Enough faith to keep away fear.

Enough wisdom to make each day better and better.

· · · · · · ·

"The highest reward for a person's toil is not what they get for it, but what they become by it."

— John Ruskin - English Art Critic (1819-1900)

There is so much about life that we don't understand. If you spend all of your time trying to figure out why this happened and that didn't happen, you're going to live a very frustrated and unsatisfied life. Having a negative attitude and choosing to be unhappy because things didn't turn out the way you hoped they would will prevent the good things from coming into your life.

"Nothing is a waste of time, if you use the experience wisely."

— Auguste Rodin - French Sculptor (1840-1917)

We are all students in a school called "Life." Who we are is the result of who we are becoming, through how we are reacting to what happens to us. The positive and negative experiences you've gone through and are going through, have created the person you are today. Who, what, when, where, and how you are is the result of everything you have learned IN LIFE SCHOOL.

"Mistakes are painful when they happen, but years later a collection of mistakes is what is called experience."

— Denis Waitley - Author of *Psychology of Success*

171

COURSE TEN

Going Through Stormy Days

"If you will call your troubles experiences, and remember that
every experience develops some latent force within you, you
will grow vigorous and happy, however adverse your
circumstances may seem to be."
— John Heywood - Playwright, *The Play of Love* (1497-1580)

Why would you leave the safety of the shoreline if it were not
for your faith in the boat under your feet? When things seem
to be sailing along smoothly, the weather can suddenly change
and make a turn for the worse. When the sea gets rough and
the storm winds blow, we grip the ship's wheel in fear as we look
back at the security of the distant shore. Before you know it, the
boat you had so much faith in is taking on water, the powerful
sails are tearing, and the mast breaks from stress and strain.

"When we long for life without difficulties, remind us that the
mighty oak grows strong in contrary winds, and diamonds
are made from extreme pressure."
— Rev. Peter Marshall - Senate Chaplain (1902-1967)

Sometimes you have to go through a storm in order to get to
where the sun is shining. Strong winds, rain, lightning, and snow,
are a natural part of nature. They all have a purpose and are used

for changing life's weather. You can't have clear and sunny weather without the rains that cleanse the skies.

"Why is this happening to me? Why am I having such a difficult time? One answer is that life is supposed to be difficult! It's what enables us to grow. Remember, earth is not heaven!"
— Rick Warren - Pastor, Author of *The Purpose Driven Life*

Yet too often we choose to run from the rain and protect ourselves from the lightening within the dark clouds. Yet when you realize that it's raining because you need to grow, you'll embrace the opportunities for change within the seasonal storms of life.

"It's in darkness that you find the light. It is in the storm that you find peace. It is in sorrow that you find joy, because life is a paradox and a polarity."
— The Spiritual Light Teachings of *Silver Birch*

All of us are sometimes overwhelmed by the crushing waves of disappointment, illness, conflict, hopelessness, depression, financial difficulties, and personal problems. These times are when you stare into the depths of your soul and decide to sail forward in fear or faith. We often call out to God and ask Him to help us, whether we believe in Him or not! When you're going through hard and challenging times and you wonder where God is, remember that the teacher is always quiet during a test.

"You'll have bad times, but they'll always wake you up to the good stuff you were not paying attention to."
— *Good Will Hunting* movie 1997

174

Forgive, leave the past behind, learn from your experience, and be grateful for all you have today. When you do this, the storms that were meant to sink you will float you onto newly inspired shores. You can only gain control of the wind when you release the sails and let go of the rudder. You don't have to look very far to see someone who has experienced something more painful or has gone through something much worse than you have! Compassion, gratitude, kindness, and love heal all wounds and turns your brokenness into wholeness.

"I will love the light for it shows me the way, yet I will endure the darkness, because it shows me the stars."
— Og Mandino - Author of *Mission: Success!* (1923–1996)

When the storm passes and the skies clear, it leaves behind a renewed sense of gratitude. We discover a part of us that we only get in touch with during the difficult times in our life. It brings out feelings that were hidden deep inside our false sense of self-confidence, until it is shaken to the surface by the power of the experience. Without the storms in our life, we wouldn't appreciate and enjoy the good weather!

"We cannot choose our external circumstances, yet we can always choose how to respond to them."
— Epictetus - Greek Philosopher (55AD-135AD)

• • • • • • •

When I was going through a very tough and challenging time, I reached down deep within my soul and wrote this song called...

TRUST

More now, than ever before,

I need more TRUST in my world.

Good times and bad times, in life will come.

Learning life's lessons through struggles I endure.

Growing stronger, wiser, better than before.

When my world inside is crumbling down.

I feel like I can't keep my feet on the ground.

I regret I didn't do what I could, would, and should.

Life is working all things, together for my good.

More now than ever before,

I need more FAITH in my world.

Trials and tribulations, part of my education.

Life is the potter, I am the clay.

Molding, changing, and teaching me.

Lead me by the still waters, through this valley of stress.

Help me swim to the surface, to take another breath.

Choosing to learn from what I'm going through.

Changes my worry to wisdom, my complaining to gratitude.

More now than ever before,

I need more HOPE in my world.

How I live through my test is my testimony.

When I get hit by life's painful darts,

My attitude shows "who I am" in my heart.

I reap what I sow by what I say and do.
Life is pruning my branches that are not bearing fruit.
I have the choice to think positive or negatively.
How I go through my problems, show me what I believe.

More now than ever before,
I need more LOVE in my world.
What do I profit in this world, if I lose my own soul?
I was born to live my life, happy and free.
With love, peace, joy, and prosperity.
Life should be great and getting better every day.

How am I living my life?
Am I really living my life?
How are you living your life?
Are you really living your life?

· · · · · · ·

"I'd always believed that a life of quality, enjoyment, and
wisdom were my human birthright. I never suspected that I
would have to learn how to live. That there were specific dis-
ciplines and ways of seeing the world I had to master before I
could awaken to a simple, happy, uncomplicated life."
— Dan Millman - Author of *The Way of the Peaceful Warrior*

Some things can only be learned during the battle, the storm,
the fire, and the flood. When the eagle faces strong winds, he
stretches his wings, rising above the bad weather. He doesn't
fight against it or struggle through it; he flows with it, allowing
the winds to take him where they want him to go. While ter-

177

rible weather rages below, the eagle soars peacefully and gracefully, high above the dark and stormy clouds.

> "Character cannot be developed in ease and quiet. Only
> through experience of trial and suffering can the soul be
> strengthened, ambition inspired, and success achieved."
> — Helen Keller - Blind Author of *Light In My Darkness* (1880-1968)

When the storms of unhappiness and disappointment come into your life, how do you handle them? Do you rise above them or do you allow the destructive powers of complaining to blow away your peace, love, joy, gratitude, and positive attitude?

> "Our finest moments are most likely to occur when we are
> feeling deeply uncomfortable, unhappy, or unfulfilled. For it
> is only in such moments, propelled by our discomfort,
> that we are likely to step out of our ruts and start
> searching for different ways or truer answers."
> — M. Scott Peck - Author of *The Road Less Traveled* (1936-2005)

· · · · · · ·

This is a letter I posted on Facebook to everyone living in the area of my hometown, Point Pleasant Beach, New Jersey, the day after they took a direct hit from "Hurricane Sandy" on October 29, 2012…

I hope you'll find COMFORT in the storm, during your wet, cold, and rainy days. POSITIVE WORDS, when negative thoughts and feelings flood your mind with sadness and losses. HUGS, when spirits become sad, worried, and weak.

LAUGHTER, to fill your heart when you need to shake off the sadness and depression. SUNSHINE, to warm your heart, home, and neighborhood. RAINBOWS, to replace the clouds, winds, and storm surge. BEAUTY, for your eyes to focus on when all you can see is the ugliness of destruction. FRIENDS, to help you with everything you need. STRENGTH, for when you doubt and cry out, "Why is this happening to me?" FAITH, to know that God isn't to blame and did not do this to you! HOPE, so you can believe that one day life will be even better than before. COURAGE, to know it will all be okay, while you are finding the power to deal with one more day of difficulties. PATIENCE, to know that today there are things you can't change and tomorrow will bring opportunities for the things you can. LOVE AND JOY, to help you deal with challenging situations, as you watch the muddy flood waters recede. BELIEF, that all of the real stuff you need will be replaced. GRATITUDE, for the life you are still living, no matter what you see, think, and feel... May this help you in some small way on your journey of recovery.

This is a Facebook comment sent to me from a hometown friend, in response to the above post and his family's experience in this great storm... "I have no phone including cells, no TV, no electric, just a radio. Candles for light at night, massive destruction along the Point Pleasant Beach, Bay Head and Mantoloking coastlines. Houses upside down, ocean front homes floating in Barnegat Bay, several are just gone! The houses that weren't destroyed are damaged and flooded. Natural Gas spewing into the air from where the houses used to be, some homes burning from ignited gas leaks. Fire trucks can't get through the damaged roads to put them out. Looks like a war zone! Cars thrown up onto sand piles fifteen feet high on East Ave and Route 35. I can't even begin to explain the destruction. Absolutely crazy to see. The Shore will never be the same! My family is doing good. Say a prayer for those who lost everything, including their lives. I hope all of my Facebook friends are fine… Peace out."

· · · · · · ·

"And once the storm is over, you won't remember how you made it through, how you managed to survive. But one thing is certain. When you come out of the storm, you won't be the same person who walked in. That's what the storm is all about."
— Haruki Murakami - Author of *After Dark*

We are all in the process of recovering from something… loneliness, betrayal, regret, guilt, loss, stress, dysfunctional relationships, disappointments, or? Don't let your tragedy become your identity. Don't allow the pains of the past to become your suffering in the present. Every time you bring up the negative things from the past, your emotional subconscious mind relives the experiences and you feel the same uncomfortable feelings all over again!

"Life is not about waiting for the storms to pass, it's about learning how to dance in the rain."
— Vivian Greene - Author of *Good Mourning*

New beginnings are often disguised as painful endings. We can be so tortured by what was and so at peace with accepting what is. May the love and laughter you find in your tomorrows wipe away the pain you find in your yesterdays. Most people think it's the holding on that makes you strong. Yet the wise ones know it's in the letting go. Always remember this ancient proverb… "This too shall pass."

"Opposition is a natural part of life. Just as we develop our physical muscles through overcoming opposition such as lifting weights, we develop our character muscles by overcoming challenges and adversity."
— Stephen Covey - Author of *The 7 Habits of Highly Effective People* (1932-2012)

COURSE ELEVEN

Turning Problems Into Possibilities

Rise… refuse to stay down. For it is in the middle of misery that so much becomes clear. Our greatest successes are not in never falling, but in getting up every time we fall. For it is through our weaknesses that we gain our power, and from our fears that we grow in faith. Choose to make a conscious decision to stop doing the things that drag you down and pull you under! Replace them with feelings, thoughts, words, and actions that lift you up toward your greatest and highest good.

Don't let what you cannot do interfere with what you can do. When your passion and purpose is greater than your fears and excuses, you'll find a way to make things happen. You can drive your car in total darkness, with only being able to see as far ahead as the end of your headlights. Life is like that. We can only see so far ahead into the future and so far behind into the past. When you hit the wall and feel like there is no place to go, remember that the wall is usually there for a reason.

"When you come to the edge of all the light you know and are about to step off into the darkness of the unknown, faith is

knowing one of two things will happen. There will be something solid to stand on or you will be taught to fly."
— Barbara Winter - Author of *Making a Living Without a Job*

SOMETIMES GOOD THINGS HAVE TO FALL APART...
so better things can come together. You will find there are inspired gains within your losses and new beginnings inside your
endings. Often the breakdown comes before the breakthrough.
It is like going into a spiritual, emotional, and mental gym.
Your muscles have to be exercised and become sore in order for
them to become stronger. We are all "wronging our way toward
right-ness."

"Perhaps our eyes need to be washed by our tears once in a
while, so that we can see life with a clearer view again."
— Alex Tan Zhixiang - Singaporean Political Activist

On her forty-fifth birthday, Regina Brett, cancer survivor, single
parent, and author of *God Never Blinks,* wrote *The 45 Lessons
Life Taught Me* for her newspaper column. Here is some of her
advice that touched my heart, mind, and soul...

* However good or bad a situation is, it will change.

* When in doubt, just take the next small step.

* You don't have to win every argument. Agree to disagree.

* Forgive everyone everything. Life is too short to waste
  time hating anyone.

* Don't compare your life to others; you have no idea what
  their journey is all about.

If we dealt with our problems when they were seeds and didn't allow them to turn into weeds, we would have a more bountiful harvest in our life. The wise use their past experiences to grow new leaves onto their tree of life. When life gives you crap, use it for fertilizer and grow a fruit-full-life.

"Be the master of your fate, not the slave of your problems."
— Marinela Reka - Author of *A Little Whisper*

The messes don't clean themselves up! You can't do it alone. We all need help with the cleanup process by getting assistance from life coaches, books, God, seminars, healers, classes, therapists, friends, family, and mentors. They will help you turn the snail pace into the fast pace, actualization into materialization!

Here is a list of some of the bad things I have experienced in my life. As a result of growing through them, I have become a better, wiser, and more empowered person. I believe that everything I have gone through including losing my father early in my life, financial losses, family issues, being robbed, the recession, a broken heart, the real estate market crash, a tax audit, injuries, bankruptcy, people dying, car accidents, identity theft, homelessness, unemployment, a near death experience, sickness, depression, failed relationships, and divorce, have molded me into who and what I am today.

"Turn your wounds into wisdom."
— Oprah Winfrey - OWN TV

Please don't get me wrong. I have lived and am living a great life! Bad things happen to good people. Stuff happens along the way that is out of our control, yet we can control how we go through it and whom we become as a result of it. Wounds will always hurt. The lessons are always in the healing process. For right below emptiness, loss, suffering, and failure, lies fulfillment, gain, enjoyment, and success.

"Of course there will be problems in life. Earth is a place where you are presented with difficulties, frustrations, obstacles and handicaps. The whole purpose of earthly existence is to meet conditions that are a challenge to the evolving spirit."
— The Spiritual Light Teachings of *Silver Birch*

It isn't your problems and challenges that define who you are, but how you react and recover from them. Problems won't disappear or turn into opportunities unless you take action to deal with them. It's okay when you take two steps forward and one step back. When you do that three times, you are still three steps ahead of where you started! It's all about taking small steps in the right direction, inch by inch, moment by moment, action into reaction. The inches eventually add up to feet, yards, and miles of action, going in the right direction.

The legendary sex symbol and movie actress, Marilyn Monroe, expressed it this way… "No matter what, you're going to mess up sometimes; it's a universal truth. Just because you fail once doesn't mean you're gonna fail at everything. Keep trying, hold on, and always believe in yourself. So keep smiling because life's a beautiful thing and there's so much to smile about."

We are all learning from the successes and failures, the excellent and awful, the happy and depressing, and the encouraging and discouraging experiences we have gone through and are going through IN LIFE SCHOOL. We love and we hate, we do right and we do wrong, we make good choices and poor choices every day of our lives!

> "I am not a product of my circumstances.
>
> I am a product of my decisions."
>
> — Stephen Covey - Author of *The Speed of Trust* (1932-2012)

How you react in the problem determines how long it will take for you to get out of the problem and into the solution. Disappointments can turn into inspired direction, weaknesses into new strength, and mistakes into valuable lessons. What you get is not nearly as important as whom you become.

> "Be still and listen for the instructions,
>
> instead of begging for the direction!"
>
> — Iyanla Vanzant - Author of *Peace From Broken Pieces*

PAIN WITH A PURPOSE, LIFE ISN'T FAIR... Yet sometimes pain, bad things, and unfairness, happen to us for a good reason. The challenge for every one of us is to see why it is happening even when we can't understand why it's happening. Our challenge is to embrace the learning experience with a positive attitude, in some way, somehow, no matter what! Just breathe...

"The universe, could only proceed from the dominion of an intelligent and powerful being. Trials are medicines which our gracious and wise Physician prescribes, because we need them and He proportions the frequency and weight of them to what the case requires."

— Isaac Newton - "Father of Modern Science" (1642-1727)

· · · · · · ·

SOMETIMES THINGS GO WRONG… I woke up to this beautiful morning and made a hot cup of coffee. While setting it down on my desk, I knocked it over and spilled it on everything! Before I reacted, I paused and embraced this inspired thought, "Let me choose to feel grateful for having a cup of coffee to spill." I cleaned up the mess, turned on my computer, and it wouldn't work. Life is a constant learning experience full of challenges and tests.

Since my computer wasn't working, I decided to clean the house. As I was cleaning the bathroom, I opened the cabinet door under the sink, leaned over, and grabbed another rag. As I was reaching, I lost my balance, grabbed the cabinet door, and ripped the hinges out of the wood frame. The screws tore out, so I figured that repairing it would be a simple job. While putting the screws back in, I broke two screws and discovered that the hinges were bent. While trying to straighten the hinges, I cracked one of them in half! I now had a useless hinge, a plugged screw hole, and a broken door.

My patience was now wearing very, very thin! I reached deep down inside myself and found the strength to control my emotions in a positive way. I knew that remaining calm about my challenging situation was my only healthy and constructive choice. No matter what, I had to go through the experience of fixing it, so deciding not to stress out was my best decision.

I found some washers, larger screws, and a hinge. I drilled some new holes, got the door to open and close, and successfully finished the repair. With all things considered, I felt really good about fixing the problem in a peaceful manner, without losing my patience and totally freaking out!

As I went about my day, I reflected on how I somehow managed to find a lesson, even in this emotionally challenging and broken experience. Life is a small percentage of what happens to us that we can't control and a bigger percentage of how we react and respond to the things we can. The choice is always ours for the making or the breaking.

· · · · · · ·

My favorite author is Og Mandino. I have read all of his books. He wrote the bestseller *The Greatest Salesman in the World*. Here is one of his pearls of wisdom… "Search for the seed of good in every adversity. Stars may be seen from the bottom of a deep well, when they cannot be discerned from the mountaintop. So will you learn things in adversity, that you would never have discovered without trouble."

Change comes in the right season. All seeds grow during their chosen time of the year. Everything happens for good, in its perfect timing of planting, growth, change, and harvest.

· · · · · · ·

THE FOUR SEASONS OF A TREE

There was a man who had four sons. He wanted his sons to learn not to judge things too quickly, so he sent them each on a quest, in turn, to go and look at a pear tree a great distance away. The first son went in the winter, the second in spring, the third in summer, and the youngest son in the fall.

When they had all gone and come back, he called them together to describe what they each had seen. The first son said that the tree was ugly, bent, and twisted. The second son said no, it was covered with green buds and full of promise. The third son disagreed. He said it was laden with blossoms that smelled so sweet and looked so beautiful, and it was the most graceful thing he had ever seen. The last son disagreed with all of them. He said it was ripe and drooping with fruit, full of life and fulfillment.

The man then explained to his sons that they were all right because they had each seen but only one season in the tree's life. He told them that you cannot judge a tree or a person by only one season in his or her life. The essence of who we are, the pleasure, joy, and love that comes from life can only be measured at the end, when all the seasons are up. If you give up when it's winter, then you will miss the promise of your spring, the beauty of your summer, and fulfillment of your fall.

The moral of this story is... Don't let the pain of one season destroy the joy of all the rest.

· · · · · · ·

Every event and season in life has a reason and offers a potential harvest of wisdom. It is up to you whether you pick the fruit from your tree of life or let it rot on your branches. Seeds of love, held in fear inside one's hand, can never sprout and be planted in your field of dreams. One must trust the natural order of life and cast your seeds where they can grow into an abundant crop and be shared and enjoyed by all. No good tree produces rotten fruit and no bad tree produces good fruit. A tree is known by its fruit. What kind of fruit are you bringing forth into your life?

· · · · · · ·

OUR BIGGEST LESSONS... come from the small things we experience in our daily lives. Today I locked myself out of my house! A repair man rang the front door bell and I stepped outside to let him in the garage, while closing the door behind me. When I tried to get back into the house, I realized I had locked myself out!

My first reaction was, "How many times have I told myself to get a hide-a-key in case this happened!" My next response was, "This is a test. Do not get mad or frustrated. I need to respond in a positive way and believe I can get back inside the house."

191

Anger, frustration, and irritation were knocking on my emotional door, and I was refusing to answer it.

I focused and thought that perhaps the upstairs window in my home office was not closed all of the way. So I got a ladder, climbed onto the slippery roof, pulled off the screen, and tugged on the sliding glass window... it opened, yes! I carefully crawled inside the window, and opened the front door. I was calm, in a positive emotional state, and felt like I had learned something powerful as a result of my problematic challenge.

The choice to react in a positive or a negative way to what is happening in my life is always up to me. Since I was already on the roof, I decided to take advantage of the situation and clean the outside of my dirty windows. Now I can see much clearer and I have a new perspective on life. I took control of my emotions and decided not to stress out or flip out, which gave me the state of mind to figure it out! I passed the test, moved on to a higher place, and grew from my inspirational experience. Next lesson...

· · · · · · ·

PROSPERITY AND ADVERSITY... are just two of the tools that life uses to teach us how to change and gain wisdom, through the valuable lessons they give us. Life never promised us a rose garden and even roses have thorns!

"In life, the things that go wrong are often the very things that lead to other things going right."
— Arianna Huffington - Founder of *The Huffington Post*

What the caterpillar thinks is the end of its life, the butterfly experiences as a new beginning. It's never about the circumstances around you, yet it's always about who and what those circumstances are transforming you into. The dark place you may be in is not where you have to stay! Decide to fail forward and never look downward, as you are rising upward to a higher place of being.

· · · · · · ·

THE BUTTERFLY'S STRUGGLE

A man found a butterfly cocoon. One day a small opening appeared. He sat and watched the butterfly for several hours as it struggled to force its body through that little hole. Then it seemed to stop making any progress. It appeared as if it had gotten as far as it could, and it couldn't go any further.

So the man decided to help the butterfly. He took a pair of scissors and snipped off the remaining bit of the cocoon. The butterfly then emerged easily. But it had a swollen body and small shriveled wings.

The man continued to watch the butterfly because he expected that at any moment, the wings would enlarge and expand to be able to support the body. Neither happened! In fact, the butterfly spent the rest of its life crawling around with a swollen body and shriveled wings. It never was able to fly!

What the man in his kindness and haste did not understand was that the restricting cocoon and the struggle required for the butterfly to get through the tiny opening, were life's way of forcing fluid from the body of the butterfly into its wings, so it would be ready for flight once it achieved its freedom from the cocoon.

Sometimes struggles and problems are exactly what we need in our lives. If life allowed us to go through it without any obstacles or challenges, it would cripple us! We could never get the opportunity to become as strong as we should have gotten. We would never get the chance to turn our struggles into opportunities and our weakness into strength, so we could be powerful enough to fly!

· · · · · · ·

Life lessons are the nuggets of gold, diamonds, rubies, and emeralds, which make us wealthy in wisdom and truth. A gem cannot be polished without friction and a person cannot be perfected without trials. The rubbing of conflicts and challenges against our gem qualities, is what cuts and polishes us into a fine precious jewel.

"There are no consequences other than those we create. Each time you forget that life is a reflection of your actions, you get a reminder."
— Jacob Liberman - Author of *Wisdom From An Empty Mind*

· · · · · · ·

DON'T QUIT

When things go wrong, as they sometimes will,
When the road you're trudging seems all up hill.
When the funds are low, and the debts are high,
And you want to smile, but you have to sigh.

When life is pressing you down a bit,
Rest if you must, but don't you quit.
Life is queer with twists and turns,
As every one of us sometimes learns.

And many a failure turns about,
When we might have won had we stuck it out.
Don't give up though the pace seems slow,
You may succeed with another blow.

Success is failure turned inside out,
The silver tint of the clouds of doubt.
And you never can tell how close you are,
It may be near when it seems so far.

So stick to the fight when you're hardest hit,
It's when things seem worse, that you must not quit.

• • • • • • •

If there are 1000 steps within your personal journey and you haven't reached your destination after taking 900 of them, don't feel like the journey has been a failure. Our life has steps that look the same, whether we are going forward or backward on the path of divine inspiration.

195

"Nothing is impossible. The word itself says, I'm possible."

—Audrey Hepburn - Legendary Film Actress (1929-1993)

Have faith in yourself. Press onward and upward. The rewards are generally at the end of an effort, not at its humble beginnings. Keep it positive and use every adversity and challenge as a learning experience! You must have a great relationship with your "Now" in order to love and enjoy life!

· · · · · · ·

AND GOD SAID NO

by Claudia Minden Weisz -
The mother of a Rett syndrome child

I asked God to take away my pride. And God said, "No." He said it was not for Him to take away, but for me to give up.

I asked God to make my handicapped child whole. And God said, "No." He said her spirit was whole, her body was only temporary.

I asked God to grant me patience. And God said, "No." He said patience is a by-product of tribulations. It isn't granted, it is earned.

I asked God to give me happiness. And God said, "No." He said He gives me blessings, happiness is up to me.

I asked God to spare me pain. And God said, "No." He said suffering draws me apart from worldly cares and brings me closer to Him.

I asked God to make my spirit grow. And God said, "No." He said I must grow on my own. But He will prune me to make me fruitful.

I asked for all things that I might enjoy life. And God said, "No." He said He will give me life, that I may enjoy all things.

I ask God to help me love others, as much as He loves me. And God said, "Ah, finally you have the idea!"

· · · · · · ·

Nobody lives a problem free, perfect life! No matter how it looks on the outside, no one lives without pain and stress. When you see the big house, the fancy car, the successful job, and wealth, it doesn't spare their owner from personal challenges in his or her life. The only way to get through the learning, changing, and growing process is to spend more time in the solution than in the problem. Sarah Breathnach, in her book *Simple Abundance,* said it best… "When we choose not to focus on what is missing from our lives, but are grateful for the abundance that's present, we experience heaven on earth."

Do not covet your neighbor's life! Don't let appearances fool you into being jealous about someone else's life and wishing you were them. For the outer world doesn't always reflect the inner person. We all experience fears, insecurities, blessings, and successes. Take the time to tend your own garden and see that everyone's yard has bees that sting and flowers that are full of beauty.

"It's a sad man, my friend, who's living in his own skin and can't stand the company. When it comes to luck, you make your own. Success makes life easier, but it doesn't make living easier."

— Bruce Springsteen - Singer, Songwriter "The Boss"

What are you doing? Are you focusing on what is good in your life or what is bad? Are you looking at the cup of life as half-empty or half-full? Will you transform your "What ifs?" into your "Now whats?" Are you still living in the past, or are you excited and hopeful about the future? Are your thoughts filled with what you want or what you really need? Do you have to lose it in order to become grateful for what you already have? Do you need to go around the mountain again in order to get where you want to be? Will you make the same mistakes again or will you learn the lessons and move forward to a better place?

"Never forget that failure isn't bad, failure isn't final. Don't let the fear of failure stop you from achieving the success you deserve. If you're struggling, keep hustling. Keep taking at least one big action step each day."

— Craig Ballantyne - Author of *How To Set Goals*

• • • • • • •

A CALL TO ACTION

What personal, mental, emotional, spiritual, physical, or financial challenges are you going through today? What are you learning from the experiences? Are they making you a better or a bitter person?

Personal? _____

_____

_____.

Mental? _____

_____

_____.

Emotional? _____

_____

_____.

Spiritual? _____

_____

_____.

Physical? _____

_____

_____.

Financial? _____

_____

_____.

Excuse me… you're addressing my past; I don't live there anymore! I have left my yesterdays behind, taking with me all of the good and inspired wisdom I have paid so dearly for. I am making a promise to myself to stop letting my past failures rob me of today's blessings, by stealing from me the possibilities within my present. I have listened to my old voice and have been stuck in my old story for far too long! My book of life is open and I am writing an inspirational story on its blank pages. I am believing that all things are working out for my good. I am loving and taking good care of myself, for I can't give to the world something I don't already have. I am using the lessons I have learned from my past, to live my best life today. I feel enthusiastic about my life, when I say these words to myself… "Life is great and getting better every day."

COURSE TWELVE

Everything Is Happening For A Reason

Everything happens for a reason, when I choose to plant my experience like a seed and then tend and water my "garden of life" with gratitude, positive thinking, faith, hope, and love. Everything happens for a reason, with the intention of teaching us life lessons, while directing us forward toward inspired growth and change. Everything happens for a reason, when you seek the purpose within why things are happening to you.

Melody Beattie, author of *Journey To The Heart,* wrote… "It doesn't take as much faith to believe that everything happens for a reason, as it does to embrace the belief, that I am who and where I am now; today; for a reason. Even if I don't know what that reason is and even if I don't particularly like who or where I am today."

LOOK FOR THE GOOD… Life is an interpretive experience. What happens is less important than how we respond to our circumstances. I know all of us have gone through things that when we looked at what was happening to us we said, "If everything happens for a reason, there has got to be one hell of a reason for this!" A recent study of "Triumphant Survivors" showed that these individuals who overcame adversity emerged strengthened, renewed, and shared the ability to discover good in every situation.

> "Suffering is part of our training program for becoming wise. Healing does not mean going back to the way things were before, but rather allowing what is now to move us closer to God. I see my life as an unfolding set of opportunities to awaken."
> — Ram Dass – Author of *Be Here Now*

· · · · · · ·

My best friend Pam was forty-seven years young when she got the shocking news of her cancer diagnosis. What wasn't included in the doctor's prognosis was who she was in her heart, mind, and soul. After spending months in the hospital recovering from her major, cutting-edge surgery, the doctors said she had only six months or less to live.

They advised her to go home and put her affairs in order. From that day forward she set her life goals, which included making it to her 50th Birthday Party. The celebration was only thirty-six months away, and she wasn't going to miss it!

Pam was determined to get every ounce of joy out of her present reality, despite the circumstances that looked so bad. Instead of drowning in a sea of sorrow, Pam chose to swim in an ocean of peace and hope. She displayed the most amazing attitude and decided not to cry a river of tears or ask the unanswerable question, "Why is this happening to me?"

"Nobody is really free until they are ready to live with their own death. Every man or woman's life ends the same way. It is only the details of how they lived and how they died, that distinguish one person from another."
— Ernest Hemingway - Author of *For Whom The Bell Tolls* (1899-1961)

Pam found the amazing courage to face her fate and the wisdom to ponder its meaning. She found the best in what she was going through, while inspiring everyone around her to find the good in what they were experiencing. People complain about growing old until the gift of living one more year is taken away from them.

"And in the end, it's not the years in your life that count, it's the life in your years."
— Abraham Lincoln - Civil War President (1809-1865)

I knew she was living her miracle, as I read her handmade party invitation…

"You are invited to my 50th Birthday Party, as I look forward to sharing this milestone of living our lives together." She had beat the odds and proved the doctors wrong! Her party wasn't about her dying, but about her joy of living and the love she shared with everyone around her.

More than two hundred people came to be a special part of her "life celebration." They arrived with smiles as they kissed and thanked her for giving them the gift of her friendship, love, and caring. We danced to an amazing band, laughed at old stories, drank from the open bar, ate delicious food, and celebrated the joy of being alive. Man, was it a great party! Like life, it seemed the evening was over before it began. It turned out to be a precious gift for everyone, as we were reminded to enjoy the "Gift of Life" in the present. Leave it to Pam to turn her sickness into a healthy, loving, and positive experience.

It had been several months since the birthday party and after a recent phone conversation with Pam, my intuition told me to fly back to Santa Barbara, sensing this may be the last time we would hang out together. So I packed my bags, boarded the plane and returned to help my best friend with her transition to a higher place.

The inspiration for writing my song "Everything Happens for a Reason," which inspired me to write this book, came to me while I was sitting with Pam under her avocado tree. For many years, we loved to sit under its wise old limbs, where we laughed, cried, and drank wine, while openly sharing everything that was going on in our lives. Yet this time together was very different. With oxygen tubes in her nose and only eighty pounds of her beautiful self left to hug, Pam had received a recent terminal cancer diagnosis…

EVERYTHING HAPPENS FOR A REASON

Everything happens for a reason, you're telling me,
My life keeps getting better and better, cause you're with me.
I love my life, things are great, thanks for loving me,
I celebrate my life, you with me.

We met worlds away, yet you have never been very far,
You know who I am and I love you, just the way you are.
You are a light to me, good advice, always there for me.

I'm so inspired by your life, love never ends,
I'm so blessed to have you in my life, my friend.

A time to be born, a time to die,
A time to laugh, a time to cry.
Come and help me try and catch the wind.
Life's a gift we've all been given,
Everybody dies, are you really livin?
Change your thinking, Change your world.

Life goes on and on, in a higher place, where souls are free,
Full of crystals and rainbows, God's love eternally.
There will be no more pain, spread your wings and fly,
butterflies on the breeze.
I'm so inspired by your life, love never ends,
I'm so blessed to have you in my life, my friend.

The healing comes when your blind eye sees,
The lessons we learn, through forgiving me.
Our hearts get drunk, drinking love.
Life's a gift we've all been given,
Everybody dies, are you really livin?
Change your thinking, Change your world.

Everything happens for a reason, you're telling me,
My life keeps getting better and better, cause you're with me.
I love my life, things are great, thanks for loving me,
We celebrate our lives, under your avocado tree.

· · · · · · ·

We had known each other since we were hippie teenagers, growing up in a small New Jersey beach town in the 70's. I had very long, sun-bleached curly hair that hung down to the middle of my back. We joked about her having gray hair and how I was thankful for every white hair I still had left! We helped each other when things were good and when there were tough times. We always told each other that we would be "Friends for life."

I was playing all of my original songs that she knew and loved, as she lay in bed listening and medicating for her pain. She turned to me and asked, "Do you think I am dying?" and I replied, "It looks like dying to me!" Being the creative soul that she was, she just had to share with me a poetic essay she'd written in an attempt to describe her thoughts and feelings about what she was going through. I will never forget these haunting words as she read…

Ever so slowly… it creeps through the open French doors of my bedroom, traveling on the soft summer breeze, beckoning for my attention in the middle of the night. At other times, it startles me at noon, when the sun is high in the sky and life is unfolding, promising a typical day filled with breakfast, lunch and dinner, calls from friends and motherly demands, when suddenly, I'm made acutely aware that my days will never be normal again, never, ever!

This haunting sound demands my attention and stops me in my tracks, serving as a subtle reminder of my fate. Sometimes it is faint and distant and I strain to recognize it, and yet at other times, it conveys its message with bold blasts that cannot be ignored.

In all its allure, I am simply mesmerized by its call and the images it summons. Its lonely wail initially brings to mind images of foggy nights with solo lamp posts, casting veiled lights on vacant scenes from classic films.

These images conjure up feelings of longing, abandonment, unfulfilled dreams, missed opportunities, and lost love. Slowly, these feelings fade and are replaced by an intoxicating sense of wonder. Why is this constant reminder here and what does its pervasive message mean?

Is this train whistle, with all its power and promise, actually singing its strange song just for me? Is it subtly serving as a constant reminder that one day its distant call will come to me one last time and whisk me away to a place unknown and un-fathomable in its glory?

Someday, I will be a passenger on this train, taken on a ride that I did not plan and that has come far too soon. It's a ride none of us is ever prepared for, and yet I feel the need to pack my bags even though I have no ticket in my hand.

· · · · · · ·

Saying goodbye to Pam was one of the hardest things I have ever done! It seemed like no matter how hard I tried to hold them back, my words were filled with loving tears. She told me how special I was and why I needed to play my music, write this book, pursue my dreams, and be happy. She added that our friendship had always been so dear to her and we would meet again in an-other life. As I was walking away, I turned around to look at her beautiful face one more time. I knew in my spirit that this would be the last time I would ever see her on this earth.

I got the call while I was waiting for my luggage at the airport baggage claim. Pam lost her battle with cancer, yet she won the greatest victory of all… living an amazing life and loving so many people along the way. She will always live in my heart.

She passed the test of time by bringing love and beauty into life's everyday moments. She chose to see the light, where others only saw shades of gray. Pam was thankful for all she had and found different ways to give and help others. I can still hear her say with irresistible warmth, "Isn't this great!"

As Pam's friends and family members walked down to the Pacific Ocean cliffs, they each released a monarch butterfly from a paper box that said, "May your spirit soar."

The ultimate cancer in life is not living the life you want to be living because of your fears and doubts. When we all take our last breath on earth, we won't say, "Am I leaving enough behind?" We should all say, "Did I leave any life unlived?"

Helping people go through their last days puts us in touch with the priceless value of our time we still have on this earth. Bronnie Ware, is an Australian nurse who spent years caring for patients in the last three months of their lives. She put her observations into a book called *The Top Five Regrets of the Dying* where she writes about what we can learn from their dying experiences.

When she asked her patients about what they would do differently in their lives if they had the chance to do it all over again, many common themes surfaced again and again within their conversations. When people were dying, these were the top five regrets that people had on their death-beds...

1. I wish I'd had the courage to live a life true to myself, not the life others expected of me.

2. I wish I didn't work so hard.

3. I wish I'd had the courage to express my feelings.

4. I wish I had stayed in touch with my friends.

5. I wish I had let myself be happier.

It all comes down to love and relationships in the end. That is all that remains in the final weeks. Good memories of loving times and caring relationships. None of us are going to be around forever. I really like this old saying, "You will never see a U-Haul in a funeral procession." The only thing we take with us is the love within our spirit-filled soul.

When someone we love passes on, there is a longing for one more day, one more word, one more touch. But little by little, we will begin to remember not just that they died, but that they lived. And that their life gave us memories too beautiful to forget.

Dr. Elisabeth Kubler-Ross, author of *On Death and Dying*, puts it like this... "It's only when we truly know and understand that we have a limited time on earth, and that we have no way of knowing when our time is up, we will then begin to live each day to the fullest, as if it was the only one we had."

Michael Josephson, founder of The Josephson Institute, influences people around the world with amazing insights like this… "So what will matter after you take your last breath upon this earth? What will matter is not what you bought, but what you built. Not what you got, but what you gave. What will matter is not your success, but your significance. Choose to live a life that matters."

"We're here to put a dent in the universe! Remembering that you are going to die, is the best way I know to avoid the trap of thinking you have something to lose. Most important, have the courage to follow your heart and intuition."
— Steve Jobs - Co-founder of Apple Computers (1955-2011)

Mother Teresa, missionary and Nobel Peace Prize recipient, expresses it like this… "At the end of life we will be judged by I was hungry and you gave me something to eat, I was naked and you clothed me, I was homeless and you took me in. Hungry not only for bread, but hungry for love, naked not only for clothing, but naked of human dignity and respect. Homeless not only for want of a home of bricks, but homeless because of rejection."

"Your soul doesn't care what you do for a living. Your soul cares only about what you're being, while you're doing whatever you are doing."
— Neale Donald Walsch - Author of *Conversations With God*

LIFE AND DEATH ARE INSEPARABLE… for one does not exist without the other. I know that most people don't like to talk about death, yet all of us will leave this earth and transcend into the great divine mystery. Everything on this earth is born to die. According to the World Health Organization, there are approximately 7 billion people living in the world, with 56 million dying each year. Every second, 5 people are born and 2 people pass away. Each minute, 300 are born and 120 people will die. Per day, 400,000 new souls are born, and 175,000 people will take their last breaths. Every year, 140 million are born, and 60 million leave this world. In the United States every year, approximately 2.5 million people will lose their lives and 4 million new babies will come into this world.

I just watched Paul Perry's documentary film *Afterlife*. In it, he interviews Dr. Raymond Moody, author of the book *Life After Life: A study of Near Death Experiences*. His research created the new field of scientific study of people who crossed over the line and entered into the realm of the afterlife. They all described similar experiences, just like the stories that have been told throughout human history. Their physical and spiritual experiences included an out-of-body experience, traveling down a long tunnel toward a bright white light, meeting spiritual beings and relatives, a panoramic review of their life and being surrounded by transformational, divine, unconditional love.

God is love, and the most common message "near-deathers" seemed to have brought back is that the most important thing we can do in this life is to "learn how to love." They all experienced the existence and presence of God, the higher consciousness realm of supernatural beings, and they all lost their fear of dying. Dr. Moody says, "Our death is an experience of love and learning, so unique that we can't perceive it without the help of God. Perhaps at death, our life has just begun."

In his New York Times best selling book *Love Wins*, Rob Bell teaches… "Eternal life is less about a kind of time that starts when we die, and more about a quality and vitality of life now in connection to God. Eternal life doesn't start when we die, it starts now."

Everybody dies, but not everyone really lives. Life is like a vapor. Birth and death, failure and success, gaining and losing, are all part of the creation and re-creation cycles of life. We are made from the earth and will return to that from which we came. In terms of life expectancy, despite being the richest country in the world, we are ranked number twenty-six at seventy-six years. Anxiety and depression disorders are soaring in the U.S. and over 39,000 people a year commit suicide. That's over 5,000 more people a year than those who die in car accidents! The choice is yours… life or death, sadness or gladness, depression or happiness. Choose life… choose love… choose happiness… choose to live your best life today.

COURSE THIRTEEN

Taking Action

Action is the great creator.

"The big secret in life is that there is no secret. Whatever your goal, you can get there if you are willing to work. It is called massive action. Action is the gas in the tank.
Without you, the car will not run."
— Marcy Blochowiak – Author of *No Glass Ceiling, Just Blue Sky*

We are creating our own destiny. Actions speak louder than words! The difference between who you are and who you want to be is what you decide to do about it. If you want to walk on water, you have to get out of the boat.

"Knowing is not enough, we must apply.
Willingness is not enough, we must do."
— Goethe - Author of *The Sorrows of Young Werther* (1749-1832)

A thousand mile journey begins with a single step. The most challenging action is always the first, for without it, nothing happens! We go down the path of life with every step and stumble as we follow our thoughts and feelings along the road of greater understanding. The personal experiences we go through change us into who we are today.

"Every accomplishment starts with the decision to try."

— Gail Devers - Three-Time Track and Field Olympic Champion

THERE IS SO MUCH SUCCESS IN TRYING... for it is the beginning of your willingness to do something new in order to get a different result and the decision to begin taking action. We need to be human doers, as well as human beings. You can't drive a car to your dream destination unless you take it out of park, step on the gas, and steer it to where you want to go. Don't be afraid of growing slowly, for you must crawl before you can walk, walk before you can run, and run before you can fly.

"The number of times I succeed, is in direct proportion to the number of times I can fail and keep on trying."

— Tom Hopkins - Author of *"How To Master the Art of Selling"*

You must be able to describe in detail what you want out of life. If you don't, how will you know when you have it? It would be like ordering something you really wanted, but you don't know what it looks like. So when it arrives at your home, you open the package and don't know what it is! You need to do more than think, pray, and mediate about it. You have to do more than affirm, visualize, and claim it. You have to do something to create it.

Mike Dooley, author of the book *Infinite Possibilities,* sums it up in this inspiring way... "Life's not about expecting, hoping and wishing, it's about doing, being and becoming. It's about the choices you've just made, and the ones you're about to make. It's about the things you choose to say today. It's about what you're gonna do after you finish reading this."

Our actions are like pebbles thrown into the water. What we think, feel, say and do sends out ever widening circles, as their effects ripple through our daily activities.

> "Motivation is not a matter of will power,
> it's a matter of want power."
> — Paul Karasik - Cartoonist, Teacher

Reading all of the inspirational self-help books in the world does nothing and means nothing, until you put them into daily practice! Perspiration, plus inspiration, equals a new creation. When I replace "I am trying" with "I am doing and being," my words are now declaring my personal commitment to positive action. I am now beyond trying and into the process of creating successes and failures, right and wrong choices, and valuable lessons and learning experiences. As long as I don't give up, all things positive and negative will be working together for my good. Don't stop before the miracle happens. Too many people give up right before they reach their goals.

> "Thinking will not overcome fear, but action will. Aim for the moon, if you miss it, you may hit a star."
> — W. Clement Stone - Author of *The Success System That Never Fails*
> (1902-2002)

Love, faith, and fear creates who we are. Every smile reflects a heart that's beating to the music of the soul. Each thought sings a song of creation, dancing to the spirit within our mind. Act, feel and think as if you already have what you've asked for and you will have it. Don't let fear blur your spiritual focus or cloud your concentrated thought. Speak it into divine existence and receive it with gratitude and an "I Am" attitude.

"When you blow a dog whistle in the presence of skeptics, they say, 'See it doesn't work'. Meanwhile there are a hundred dogs outside your door who heard it!"

— Dr. Brian Weiss - Therapist, Author of *Many Lives, Many Masters*

We all need a power greater than ourselves to help us through the challenges of living. Can you make the sun rise or the sun set? Can you put stars into the heavens or lay down the foundations of the earth? Can you make the winds blow, the flowers bloom, or the tides turn? Did you create yourself, or did someone or something create you? Life is a mystery filled with divine wisdom and earthly needs.

"Imagination is the beginning of creation. You imagine what you desire, you will what you imagine, and at last, you create what you will."

— George Bernard Shaw - Irish Playwright, *Misalliance* (1856-1950)

Written over 2000 years ago, the New Testament Bible uses the word faith 254 times, heart 105, joy 63, light 95, love 232, wisdom 53, and wealth 18 times. I think God is trying to tell us something good, so we can live a better life.

"Heaven never helps the person who will not act."

— Sophocles - Greek Playwright, *Oedipus the King* (496 BC-406 BC)

We all ask the same internal questions… "Where did I come from?"… "What is the purpose and meaning of my life?"… "Does God really exist?"… "Is there life after death?"… The answers lie within our eternal souls and the longer we live, the more questions we get to ask. No one lives forever, at least not on this earth! So you might as well pursue your goals and dreams with positive action and unwavering faith. You have nothing to lose and everything to gain!

· · · · · · ·

FAITH IN THE UNSEEN WORLD

In a mother's womb were two babies. One asked the other, "Do you believe in life after delivery?" The other baby replies, "Why, of course I do. There has to be something after delivery. Maybe we are here to prepare ourselves for what we will be later." "Nonsense," says the other baby. "There is no life after delivery. What would that life be like?" "I don't know, but there will be more light than in here. Maybe we will walk with our legs and eat from our mouths?"

The first baby says, "That is absurd! Walking is impossible. And eating with our mouths? Ridiculous! The umbilical cord supplies us our nutrition. Life after delivery is to be excluded, because the umbilical cord is too short!" "I disagree," the other baby replies, "I think there is something and maybe it's different than it is in here."

The first replies, "No one has ever come back from there. Delivery is the end of life, and in the after-delivery it is nothing but darkness and anxiety, and it takes us nowhere." "Well, I don't know," says the other. "But certainly we will see Mother and she will take care of us."

The other baby responds passionately, "Mother? You believe in Mother? Where is she now?" With deep emotion, the other baby replies, "She is all around us. It is in her that we live. Without her there would not be this world that we live in." The first baby declares, "I don't see her, so it's only logical that she doesn't exist."

To which the other replies with a deep sense of calling, "Sometimes when you're in silence, you can hear her, you can perceive her. I believe there is a reality after delivery and we are here to prepare ourselves for that reality."

· · · · · · ·

FAITH WITHOUT ACTION... is no life at all. Don't be upset about the results you don't have because of the work you didn't do! A new computer that isn't plugged in can't help you. A new Mercedes in the garage without any gas will take you nowhere. Faith without action is an unfulfilled life, a self-created form of doubt and fear. Faith with action is an inspired and motivated life, full of blessings, love, health, and prosperity.

"We are what we repeatedly do. Excellence then is
not an act, but a habit."
—Aristotle - Greek Philosopher (384BC-322BC)

LIFE IS LIKE FISHING... In order to catch a fish, you have to pick up the pole and cast it into the waters of opportunity. If you dream of having a fish dinner, the more you cast your line into the sea of life, the greater your chances are of catching one. So our job is to believe we are going to reel in our desires by putting the bait and hook on the line. So now I must excuse myself; I have lots to do. Please tell everyone "I've gone fishing."

"When faced with a decision, many people say they are waiting for God. But I understand in most cases, God is waiting for me."
— Andy Andrews - Author of *The Noticer*

There were two farmers who hoped and prayed for rain. One of the farmers plowed his field, planted his seed, and waited in faith for the rain to fall. The other farmer did nothing, but kept on praying. Which farmer had a bountiful harvest when it rained?

Faith without action produces very little harvest, except disappointment, frustration, and emotional famine. God does all things with us and seldom totally for us. Faith is the substance of things hoped for and the belief in things not yet seen.

Theodore Roosevelt, whose face can be seen on Mount Rushmore and is considered by historians to be one of our greatest presidents, wrote this about taking action... "It is not the critic who counts, not the man who points out how the strong man stumbles, or where the doer of deeds could have done them better. The credit belongs to the man who is actually in the arena, whose face is marred by dust and sweat and blood, who strives valiantly, who errs, who comes short again and again, because there is no effort without error and shortcoming, but who does actually strive to do the deeds, who knows great enthusiasms, the great devotions, who spends himself in a worthy cause, who at the best knows in the end the triumph of high achievement, and who at the worst, if he fails, at least fails while daring greatly, so that his place shall never be with those cold and timid souls who neither know victory nor defeat."

LET YOUR FAITH... be bigger than your fears. Fear is the enemy of faith. Once your prayers are answered and you get what you want, you may begin to become afraid of losing what you now have. This is when you need to become aware of the peace and love of having something, just for your time of enjoying it. This awareness is what makes it all worth having. Nothing ever really belongs to us; we're just borrowing it. We are care-takers only for the prescribed time in which we're given to have it in our possession.

"Nothing in life is to be feared, it is only to be understood. Now is the time to understand more, so that we may fear less."
— Marie Curie - Scientist, First Woman Nobel Prize Winner (1867-1934)

When you feed your faith, you starve your fear. Enlightenment, healing, and change sometimes can only be found on the other side of pain and problems. I cheated on my fears, broke up with my doubts, got engaged to my faith, and married my dreams. Fear and faith can't stay in the same room together. Fear knocked at the door; my faith answered and no one was there.

"False Evidence Appearing Real… When I am challenged by my finances, a relationship or a major life decision, my judgment may be clouded by doubt, or confusion. Yet I know the answers are available to me, when I get worry and fear out of the way."
— *The Daily Word*

• • • • • • •

I was meditating one morning and this story manifested into my head. It's about a woman who prayed her whole life for the money she needed for all of the things she wanted to do. She believed she didn't have the finances to do them and chose to live in a mental, emotional, and spiritual state of poverty. She complained and complained that she didn't have enough money, but if she did, she would do and have everything she needed.

She prayed every day, yet she lacked the faith to believe that her prayers had been answered. She knew she had very little money in her savings account, so she never checked her balance or opened up her monthly bank statements. In frustration, she just threw the unopened letters away and went on being depressed and hoping for prosperity.

She lived paycheck to paycheck, paying everything with cash, so she would know when the money ran out! She proclaimed, that if she only had more money, she would be happy and enjoy life. She felt she was a victim and nothing good ever happened to her. She had alienated her friends and family by choosing to live a sad, miserable and unhappy life. She chose never to return their phone calls, letters, or emails.

Then one day she became very ill and ended up in the hospital. Her sister decided to visit her, even though she knew she wouldn't want to see her! After the initial negative greeting, they engaged in a cordial conversation.

The sick woman complained that her life had been wasted, that God never answered her prayers, and the universe never provided a way for her to fulfill her dreams. The sister, who was happy, prosperous and living in a big house, could not understand her sister's complaining. She exclaimed, "Wasn't your inheritance, the 500,000 dollars that Uncle James left each of us, enough money to make you happy?"

You see, the money was automatically transferred by the probate lawyers into her savings account. Yet she never showed enough faith by checking her bank balance to see whether God had answered her prayers and brought her the financial increase she was always praying for!

Too often our prayers are answered and the universe provides for our needs, yet we never think, speak, or act any differently. Even though we have what we asked for, we never believe we have received it, even after it has been given to us. You must act as if you have it and let go of your old mindset of not having and being it.

She was rich all along but chose to live a hopeless, poor and loveless life. Deposits of blessings come into our lives every day, yet too often we are not aware of them! We need to act in faith by calculating our own self-worth in love, peace, joy, and gratitude. God answers prayers. It's up to us to count our blessings and check the balance in our life account.

• • • • • • •

"Tragedies do happen. We can discover the reason, blame others, imagine how different our lives would be had they not occurred. But none of that is important, they did occur, and so be it! From there onward we must put aside the fear they awoke in us and begin to rebuild."

— Paulo Coelho - Author of *The Winner Stands Alone*

Courage is not the absence of fear, but the willingness and strength to triumph over it. The brave ones feel afraid, yet decide not to give into their fear. They do it scared and weak, knowing that the fear will pass and they'll be strengthened by their choice to take action.

Wonderful things happen when you are outside of your comfort zone, because everything you want is on the other side of fear. Martin Luther King Jr. said, "Faith is taking the first step, even when you don't see the whole staircase."

· · · · · · ·

A CALL TO ACTION

WHAT DO YOU FEAR THE MOST?

1. _____.

2. _____.

3. _____.

4. _____.

5. _____.

WHICH FEARS WILL YOU OVERCOME TODAY WITH FAITH AND CHANGE YOUR LIFE FOREVER?

Your answers will set you free...

1. _____.

2. _____.

3. _____.

4. _____.

5. _____.

· · · · · · ·

"To love is to risk not being loved in return. To hope is to risk pain. To try is to risk failure. But risk must be taken, because the greatest hazard in life is to risk nothing."

— Leo Buscaglia - Author of *Living, Loving and Learning*

LIFE GAVE ME WINGS TO FLY... and I allowed my fears to take my power of flight away. Miracles start to happen when you give as much energy to your dreams as you do to your fears! Circumstances don't change; we do! We decide to do it weak and scared, instead of not doing it because of our weakness and fear. The experience is always conditional and suffering is always optional. The biggest risk in life is not taking any chances at all. If you choose to be afraid of flying, you will never discover you can soar higher and farther than you ever dreamed you could, would, and should.

"Remember, the thoughts you think and the statements you make regarding yourself, determine your mental attitude. If you have a worthwhile objective, find the one reason why you can achieve it, rather than hundreds of reasons why you can't."
— Napoleon Hill - Author of *Think and Grow Rich* (1883-1970)

Take the leap and jump off the cliff that you've always been afraid of falling from. Rise above your circumstances, and soar like an eagle, high into the sky where you have always wanted to fly. Do what makes you feel alive and then you will soar!

"The key to success is to focus our conscious mind on things we desire, not things we fear."
— Brian Tracy - Author of *The Ultimate Success Guide*

I first heard these words of wisdom by Marianne Williamson in the movie *Coach Carter*. In her *New York Times* best-selling book *A Return to Love,* Marianne expresses these deeply inspiring truths... "Our deepest fear is not that we are inadequate. Our deepest fear is that we are powerful beyond measure. It is our light, not our darkness that most frightens us. We ask ourselves who am I to be brilliant, gorgeous, handsome, talented, and fabulous? Actually, who are you not to be?"

I was watching the Olympic Games and couldn't help being impressed by all of the amazing athletes. Whether they won or lost, their determination to give 110 percent spoke volumes to my soul. They trained as hard as their talent and abilities would allow them to. Then they showed up and gave it their all. The world was watching, the TV cameras were rolling, the crowd was cheering, and it was time to perform in the "Big Show."

"If you are making mistakes, then you are trying new things,
learning, pushing yourself, changing yourself and
changing your world."
— Neil Gaiman - Author of *Stardust*

If you take aim and fire at nothing, you are guaranteed to hit your target every time! You miss 100 percent of the shots you don't take, because you were afraid of missing them. You can't catch a wave, if you don't paddle out! You can't get on base, if you don't step up to the plate and swing the bat. You have to get in the pool, run the race, and believe you can be victorious. You must first do these things before you can experience winning a medal in the "Olympics of Life."

"Knowing is not enough, we must apply. Being willing is not
enough, we must do. Even the richest soil if left uncultivated,
will produce the rankest weeds. Iron rusts from disuse,
water loses its purity from stagnation. Even so does
inaction sap the vigor of the mind."
— Leonardo da Vinci - Renaissance Painter, Sculpture (1452-1519)

THE POWER OF ONE... The ocean is made up of single drops of water, that have joined together as one. As one person, you may not be able to solve the problems of the world, yet you can help the person the universe has put right in front of you. When one does nothing, nothing changes. Everybody has the power of one.

· · · · · · ·

I discovered this poetic inspiration on the Internet. It speaks of how we as individuals can make a difference, one thought, one feeling, one action, one day at a time...

JUST ONE

One song can spark a moment,
One flower can wake the dream.
One tree can start a forest,
One bird can herald spring.

One smile begins a friendship,
One handshake lifts a soul.
One star can guide a ship at sea,
One word can frame the goal.

One vote can change a nation,
One sunbeam lights a room.
One candle wipes out darkness,
One laugh will conquer gloom.

One step must start each journey,
One word must start each prayer.
One hope will raise our spirits,
One touch can show you care.

One voice can speak with wisdom,
One heart can know what's true.
One life can make a difference,
You see, it is up to you!

• • • • • • •

We have all had the experience of doubt and fear creeping in, ever so slowly. It turns your motivation into procrastination, your drive into a crawl. Your vision blurs, your light grows dim, and your spirit becomes discouraged. The heat of excitement, passion, and enthusiasm, begins to cool. Then through a transformation of change, positive thinking, and encouragement, your strength returns stronger, your ambition burns brighter, and your faith, hope, and love is renewed, restored, and born again.

"What this power is I cannot say; all I know is that it exists and it becomes available only when a person is in that state of mind in which they know exactly what they want and are fully determined not to quit until they find it."
— Alexander Graham Bell - Inventor of the Telephone (1847-1922)

We can do all things, think all things, feel all things and be all things, when we believe. When God is for us, nothing can be against us. We are not a failure at getting something we want, until we stop trying and start complaining. When we take action and add the letter "o" to God, it always turns into "Good."

"Nothing can stop the man or woman with the right mental attitude from achieving happiness, health and prosperity. Nothing on this earth can help the person with the wrong mental attitude achieve the opposite."
— Thomas Jefferson - Third U.S. President (1743-1826)

Henry Ford, founder of the Ford Motor Company, said it so profoundly... "If you think you can or you think you can't, either way, you are usually right. Life is a series of experiences, each of which makes us bigger. For the world was built to develop character, and we must learn that the setbacks and hardships help us in our marching onward. Failure is simply the opportunity to begin again, this time more intelligently."

"The greatest mistake you can make in your life, is to be continually fearing, that you will make a mistake."
— Elbert Hubbard - Died in the sinking of the Lusitania (1856-1915)

No matter how scared, or tired, or sick you are. No matter how lost, or confused, or desperate you become. No matter how lonely, depressed, or upset you are feeling. Do what you can do now and choose not to worry about the rest. If you just do what you can with what you have from right where you are, it will always be enough to make your life better today. Success, health, happiness, contentment, and peace are not in the future; it all already exists in the now! Go with the flow, for you will only drown in your negativity if you try to swim up stream!

"Action is a great restorer and builder of confidence. Inaction is not only the result, but the cause of fear. Perhaps the action you take will be successful; perhaps different action or adjustments will have to follow. But any action is better than no action at all."
— Norman Vincent Peale - Author of *The Power of Positive Thinking* (1898-1993)

What if you were guaranteed that all your needs would be met, and you would have everything your heart desires? Imagine possessing everything you needed to fulfill all of your ambitions and dreams. You would, of course, have to do your part and apply your time, talents, and finances toward making them happen. You would need to believe in yourself while taking action. Part of your success will be creating a plan, making goals, and working on them with passion and enthusiasm. You might even have to take some risks, do a few things you don't want to do, and sacrifice some things that are important to you!

"Instead of dwelling on the negative things that can happen, focus on the incredible gifts this opportunity can bring. Fear is like gravity, an invisible force that keeps us rooted to an experience. It's only when we let go and leap beyond the force that holds us back, that we lovingly liberate our unlimited potential."
— Panache Desai - Author of *Igniting Boundless Receiving*

. . . .

A CALL TO ACTION

How would you be living if all of your prayers, hopes, and wishes were all answered, fulfilled, and given to you?
What dreams would you choose to accomplish?

1. _____.

2. _____.

3. _____.

4. _____.

5. _____.

What would you do today, if you knew you wouldn't fail and were 100 percent guaranteed to succeed at all of your heart's desires?

1. _____.

2. _____.

3. _____.

4. _____.

5. _____.

IF TODAY WAS THE LAST DAY OF YOUR LIFE...

How would you want to live it? What would you do, what would you say, how would you think, what would you feel, whom would you call?

1. _____.

2. _____.

3. _____.

4. _____.

5. _____.

· · · · · · ·

Now, your newly inspired job is to live your life in faith, as if you already have everything you wanted, believing that in time it will manifest itself. No more waiting, hoping, or procrastinating! Your life experience is being it, thinking it, feeling it, and doing it as if your dreams, desires, and heart-felt needs are your present day reality. For everything you needed is already in your possession because you are living as if you already have it today.

"There are three types of people in the world: Those who make things happen, those who watch what happens, and those who wonder what happened."
— Nicholas Butler - 1931 Nobel Peace Prize Winner (1862-1947)

PROCRASTINATION... is when not making a decision is making a decision. It's when not taking action is taking action. Without action, nothing happens. Doing something about it changes everything. No matter how many inspiring words you read, what good will they do you if you don't act upon them?

"You may never know what results come from your actions. But if you do nothing, there will be no result."
— Gandhi - Leader of India's Independence Movement (1869-1948)

If you are like so many people who are struggling with procrastination, you will benefit from reading this only if you decide to read it now, instead of later!

· · · · · · ·

MY PROCRASTINATION

Procrastination is my weakness,
It only brings me sorrow.
I know I should give it up,
In fact, I will tomorrow!

· · · · · · ·

All of us experience this type of fear at some time in our lives. It's when we choose to do it later or tomorrow or next week that we get caught up in this unproductive behavior. The fear of failure or the responsibilities of success influence us not to try, so there will be no negative consequences for our unsuccessful actions. No action… no reaction! No success… no failure! No risk… no pain!

> "The greatest of all mistakes is to do nothing,
> because you think you can only do a little."
> — Zig Ziglar - Author of *How to Get What You Want* (1926-2012)

Tomorrow never really comes because by the time it gets here, it turns into today…

> "Don't wait until everything is just right. There will always be challenges, obstacles and less than perfect conditions. So what, get started now. With each step you take, you will grow stronger and stronger, more and more skilled, self-confident, and successful."
> — Mark Victor Hansen - Co-Author of *Chicken Soup for The Soul*

Figure out what you want and then learn how to ask for it. For it's in the knowing what to ask for, that creates what you receive. Too many people go to their graves with their art, book, music, and dreams still inside of them. Let your life become the instrument that plays your song of inspired creation.

> "All life is an experiment. Life is a series of lessons, which must be lived to be understood. The more experiments you make the better. Don't go where the path may lead; go instead where there is no path and leave a trail."
> — Ralph Waldo Emerson - Writer, *The Over-Soul* (1803-1882)

· · · · · · ·

This is a story about four people: *Everybody, Somebody, Anybody,* and *Nobody.* There was an important job to be done and *Everybody* was sure that *Somebody* would do it. *Anybody* could have done it, but *Nobody* did it. *Somebody* got angry about that because it was *Everybody's* job. *Everybody* thought *Anybody* could do it, but *Nobody* realized that *Everybody* wouldn't do it. It ended up that *Everybody* blamed *Somebody* when *Nobody* did what *Anybody* could have done!

· · · · · · ·

"Even if you are on the right track, you'll get run over
if you just sit there."
— Will Rogers - Actor, Humorist (1879-1935)

In his online article "10 Simple Truths Smart People Forget," Marc Hack writes… "Education and intelligence accomplish nothing without action. It doesn't matter if you have a genius IQ and a PhD in Quantum Physics, you can't change anything or make any sort of real-world progress without taking action. There's a huge difference between knowing how to do something and actually doing it!"

We set our goals, step toward our passions and enthusiastically climb the ladder of inspired dreams. Rung by rung, step by step, we ambitiously climb… inspired, driven, and excited about our future. Eventually we get to the top, peek over the edge, and see our dreams and desires coming true. Yet to our surprise, it turns out not to look like what we thought it would be. It doesn't feel like we thought it would feel, and we realize we haven't arrived at our goal, but a new beginning. Life and success is like that.

"Faith is daring to put your dreams to the test. It is better to try to do something and fail, than to try to do nothing and succeed."

— Dr. Robert Schuller – Televangelist, *The Hour of Power*

In the game of life… you create what you want and what you don't want! Life doesn't care what you ask for; it simply delivers to you what you focus on the most. It starts with a thought, which turns into a feeling, which produces an action; then your life becomes the reaction. It's not about whether you win or lose; it's all about what you are learning and why you are enjoying or not enjoying the game.

"Three simple rules for life: One, If you do not go after what you want, you will never have it. Two, If you do not ask, the answer will always be no. Three, If you do not step forward, you will always be in the same place."

— Nora Roberts - Romance Writer of *The Collector*

Today is the beginning of a new day, complete with 24 hours of opportunities, choices, and attitudes. A perfectly matched set of 1440 minutes. You have been given this day to use as you will. You can waste it or use it for good. What you do today is important because you are exchanging a day of your life for it. When tomorrow comes, this day will be gone forever. In its place is something that you have left behind, let it be something good. This unique gift, this one day, cannot be exchanged, replaced or refunded. Handle with care. Make the most of it. There is only one to a customer.

> "Life is not a spectator sport. If you're going to spend your whole life in the grandstand just watching what goes on, in my opinion you're wasting your life."
> — Jackie Robinson - First Black Man in Major League Baseball (1919-1972)

· · · · · · ·

A CALL TO ACTION

> "A real decision is measured by the fact that you've taken a new action. If there is no action, you haven't truly decided."
> — Tony Robbins - Self-Help Trainer, Motivational Speaker

What things can you do right now that will make a big or small difference in your life today?

1. _____.

2. _____.

3. _____.

4. _____.

5. _____.

> "We are what we repeatedly do. Excellence then is not an act, but a habit."
> — Aristotle - First Historical Scientist (384BC-322 BC)

What things do you know in your heart, mind, and soul that you should be doing but are not?

1. _____.

2. _____.

3. _____.

4. _____.

5. _____.

"Action may not always bring happiness,
but there is no happiness without action."

— Benjamin Disraeli - British Prime Minister (1804-1881)

What things have you learned by reading the *Taking Action* course?

1. _____.

2. _____.

3. _____.

4. _____.

5. _____.

"When you find your path, you must not be afraid. You need to have sufficient courage to make mistakes. Disappointment, defeat and despair are the tools God uses to show us the way."

— Paulo Coelho - Author of *The Supreme Gift*

COURSE FOURTEEN

Making A Shift

You are only one degree from where you need to be. A one percent change in your actions, makes a 100 percent difference in how you think, feel, and act. You are now permanently re-shaped, forever altered from whom you used to be. Once anything is redesigned just a little, it is completely rearranged forever. Even if you choose to go back to doing what you thought you had changed for good, you're still not the same person! You cannot unscramble an egg. Once the cooking takes place, you can never transform it back into a raw egg in the shell again.

"The moment in between what you once were, and what you are now becoming, is where the dance of life really takes place."
— Barbara De Angelis - Author of *How Did I Get Here*

Sometimes what we are doing in life is like figuring out where the pieces go in a jigsaw puzzle. We try to force pieces into places where they do not fit, even when we know they're not the right ones. If I keep doing what I have always done, I will keep getting what I have always gotten. Nothing is different until I am transformed. Only I can be the change I want to see in my world.

"The truth is that you already are what you are seeking."
— Adyashanti - Author of *Falling Into Grace*

You must let go of what you don't want in order to get what you do want. You have to let go of where you are in order to get where you want to go! There is an old saying about loving people, "If you open your hand and let them go and they stay, then it was meant to be. If you set them free and they fly away, they needed to leave and experience something that is different from being with you." There will be a missing and grieving process, yet to do anything else will only create pain and suffering, instead of peace, acceptance, love, and harmony.

· · · · · · ·

This is one of my favorite inspirational writings by Ernest Holmes, the author of *The Science of Mind*...

"She let go... without a thought or word, she let go. She let go of the fear. She let go of the judgments. She let go of the opinions swarming around her head. She let go of the committee of indecision within her. She let go of all the "right" reasons. Wholly and completely, without hesitation or worry, she just let go. She didn't ask anyone for advice. She didn't read a book on how to let go. She just let go. She let go of all the memories that held her back. She let go of all the anxiety that kept her from moving forward. She let go of the planning and all the calculations, about how to do it just right. In the space of letting go she let it all be. A small smile came over her face. A light breeze blew through her. And the sun and the moon shone forever more."

· · · · · · ·

Everyone has the strength just to give up. Sometimes it seems like it would be the easiest and smartest thing to do! Yet when you dig deep down inside and find the willpower to go on, that's where you find your real strength and courage. When you accept and let go of what you can't do for now, you become more empowered to accomplish what you can do today. You must believe in order to receive. Life is a game meant to be won by learning the next lesson and scoring the winning point.

"Courage doesn't always roar. Sometimes courage is the little voice at the end of the day that says, 'I'll try again tomorrow.'"
— Mary Anne Radmacher - Author of *Life Begins When You Do*

Taking risks brings us into the pure passion and excitement of feeling free and being truly alive. Tasting failure or setbacks brings us into the pain of the uncomfortable process of rearranging and changing. We avoid altering our behavior in favor of temporary comfort. Sometimes you have to lose something in order to gain everything.

"You can never cross the ocean unless you have the courage to lose sight of the shore."
— Christopher Columbus - Discovered "The New World" (1451-1506)

There have been times in my life when deep down inside, I knew I was going in the wrong direction! Yet even when I traveled down a dead end street, it turned out that I needed to go there to learn. Wrong turns become right turns when you turn yourself around and go in the better direction. And the amazing

241

thing is that most of the time, you don't even know where you need to be until you get there!

> "Every person is a damn fool for at least five minutes every day. Wisdom consists in not exceeding the limit."
> — Elbert Hubbard - Philosopher (1856-1915)

Once you understand why you made the decisions that put you in a place you don't like, you can then use the experiences to make better choices which will put you in a place you do like. You must be totally honest with yourself about where you are at, and where you would rather be, so you can get to where you want to go!

> "People get confused in this life about what they want, what they've done and what they think they should have because of it. Everything they think they are or did, takes hold so hard, that it won't let them see what they can be."
> — *Open Range* movie 2004

Step out of your history and into your destiny. Stop telling yourself your old story; use your past for a purpose and be present in your now. Take your "Why did I's," your "What if's," and your "How come they's," and say to your heart, mind, and soul, "Now what can I do to create good in my life today?"

Our eyes are in the front of our head because we are designed to look forward and not backwards. I am in the process of stepping into the unknown and creating my new normal. I am letting the old things pass away, and making way for the new. Sometimes we are pawns in the chess game of life and the only way we can win is by making a risky move. If you count your losses as lessons and your setbacks as comebacks, you will never lose and always gain.

"And the day came when the risk to remain tight in a bud, was more painful than the risk it took to blossom."
— Anais Nin - Author of *Mirages*

Life is one percent of what happens to you and ninety-nine percent about how you choose to react to it with your thoughts, feelings, words, and actions. We are the living sum of all of our responses to all of the things we have experienced in our life.

Small modifications made every day, will make a big difference in your life. Everyone can find one little thing he or she knows for sure she can do to make a sizable difference! Insignificant efforts will cause a significant effect when they are done persistently. Making a collective difference is the manifestation of minor things into major ones. Shifting things in your life is hard when you think of them as heavy objects. Creating something different is easy when you see them as small things accumulating into larger results.

"I can't change the direction of the wind, but I can adjust my sails to always reach my destination."
— Jimmy Dean - Country Music Singer, Actor (1928-2010)

Choose to love when you could hate. Make up your mind to forgive when you would blame. Decide to feel good when you should feel bad. Choose to be happy when you could be disappointed. Decide to be grateful when you would complain. Make up your mind to struggle for victory when you should settle for defeat!

Everything is still the same situation, yet with a simple shift in your response, you'll always get significantly different results. You simply act the way you would rather feel. This is the complete opposite of what your emotional brain and inner feelings will tell you to do. Yet when you choose these contrary actions, they will make a complete difference in how you experience life.

"Minds are like parachutes. They only function
when they are open."
— Sir James Dewar - Physicist (1842-1923)

The only person you will be living the rest of your life with is you! No one can live your life for you or give you the life you want to be living. You can never get back the life you used to have or be happy with living in the past. All you will ever have is the reality of your NOW… which in a moment becomes your PAST… and in a second turns your FUTURE into your most valuable gift… your PRESENT.

"When you stop focusing on what didn't happen and what you
don't have, and instead focus on what you want, you will live a
life full of abundance and prosperity on all levels, and the out-
comes will be better than you could have ever imagined."
— Sierra Goodman - Author of *Oceans of Inspiration*

It sure is scary when the wheels come off and you crash and burn along the highways of life. I have had this happen to me more than once! Yet each time I came to the self-realization that I can choose to fall forward, instead of backwards. That the only place I can go is inside myself to find the meaning, purpose, and lessons within my experience. Road rage, complaining, and blaming others for the accidents will only worsen your condition and won't help you with the repairs!

"Always continue the climb. It is possible for you to do whatever you choose, if you first get to know who you are and are willing to work with a power that is greater than ourselves to do it."
— Ella Wheeler Wilcox - Author of *Poems of Passion* (1850-1919)

The journey to enlightenment is a winding road, and sometimes your vehicle simply breaks down. The key is to turn your challenges into exciting opportunities, your brokenness into a new creation, and your problem into a powerful changing force. We are on the highway of life to learn, grow, and to become a better and safer motorist. With a lot of driver's education, we will all have a safe and enjoyable ride!

ENLIGHTENMENT is insight, understanding, awareness, wisdom, education, learning, knowledge, awakening, instruction, teaching, advancement, development, open-mindedness, and being in-the-light.

· · · · · · ·

The ultimate failure is in never trying!
The worst rejection is in being afraid to ask!
The deepest atheism is in not believing in yourself.
The strongest love is in loving yourself.

· · · · · · ·

"If you want to awaken all of humanity, then awaken all of yourself. If you want to eliminate the suffering in the world, then eliminate all that is dark and negative in yourself. Truly, the

greatest gift you have to give is that of your
own self-transformation."
— Lao Tzu - Sixth Century Founder of Taoism

After many years of living and learning, I have come to the realization that when things don't go my way, they're ultimately leading to my greatest and highest good. I have learned that most of the time, "Good Gifts" filled with light often come from "Bad Gifts" filled with darkness. My "What ifs" keep me living in the past and my "What nows" bring me into my action in the present. Through the awareness that I can't alter what has already happened, I have learned from the awareness that I can redesign "Who I am" and "How I am living," right now, in this moment of my today. Some people are always grumbling because roses have thorns. I'm thankful that thorns have roses.

"If you make the world better in one way, it becomes better in every way. If there is a bad taste in your mouth, spit it out instead of constantly swallowing it back."
— *Amazing Grace* movie 2006

WHEN YOU SPEAK... about what's going on in your life, you can use words to describe your situation or to transform it. You can either be declaring the way things are and making the situation more powerful or be affirming how you want things to be. We create our future according to what we choose to think, feel, and say. There is a healthy amount of talking about something, and there is the point where it's doing more harm than good. If you want to alter your circumstances, then start by changing your words.

"Talking about our problems is our greatest addiction.
Break the habit. Talk about your joys."
— Rita Schiano - Author *of Live A Flourishing Life*

SPEAK TO THE MOUNTAIN… When we talk about something we don't like or something wonderful that is happening to us, it magnifies it and makes it stronger. In order to get over it or to have more of it, you must speak to it, not just about it. You must speak and declare new things in order to start seeing different things in your life! Speak it into existence by using life-transforming words that push you toward your heartfelt desires. Choose to declare blessings and happiness, gratitude and love, health and healing. Decide to proclaim the solutions to your problems!

"Whoever says to this mountain, be removed and be cast into the sea, and does not doubt it in their heart, but believes that what they say will happen, it will be done for them."
— Jesus - *Mark 11:23*

Ever so slowly… success is a process. Focus your words on the desired results, not what you don't want in your life. If your issue is anger and resentment, don't say, "I don't want to be angry anymore!" Say to yourself and to the negative behavior, "I am peaceful, loving, and full of forgiveness." If it's unhappiness and depression you want to experience differently, speak, "I am full of happiness, joy, and gratitude."

"You have a clean slate every day you wake up. You have a chance every single morning to make that change and be the person you want to be. You just have to decide to do it. Decide today's the day. Say it, this is going to be my day."
— Brendon Burchard - Author of *Life's Golden Ticket*

When you focus on or constantly verbalize what you don't want, you get more of it! When you concentrate on and imitate the thing you do want, you become it. There are no failures in this process, only half successes. Small goals reached = Big results. The constant dripping of water has caused many floods. A little bit of love goes a long, long way.

> "Don't use your words to describe the situation,
> use your words to change the situation."
> — Joel Osteen - Televangelist, Author of *Your Best Life Now*

EVERY WORD IS A SEED... which produces a harvest in your future. When we speak and plant words of love and positive blessings, we experience a harvest of love and blessings. When we speak words of defeat and failure, those seeds produce defeat and failure. The life you are living today is the harvest from the word seeds you planted in your past. You can begin right now to plant seeds of blessings, strength, gratitude, forgiveness, love, victory, and joy. Then in time and season, you will reap a bountiful harvest.

> "Our words pass through three gates: At the first gate, we ask
> ourselves, are these words true? At the second gate, we ask,
> are they necessary? At the third gate, we ask, are they kind?"
> — Eknath Easwaran - Author of *Words to Live By* (1910-1999)

· · · · · · ·

WHAT IS AN AFFIRMATION? Affirmations talk to the subconscious soul. They are the words we say to ourselves on the inside and speak out loud to ourselves and others which encourage, strengthen, and create a powerful positive mindset. They can be said any way you like. Yet they require being said over and over again throughout the day, until they become your newly inspired way of thinking. Here are a few of the affirmations I say to myself...

I can be, do, and have anything I want in life.
I am blessed, so I can be a blessing to others.
I am a good and loving person.
I am radiating happiness to everyone I meet.
I have everything I need to live a great life today.
I am grateful for everything in my life.
I am worthy, wealthy, healthy, and wise.
I am attracting the right people, places, and things into my life.
I deserve to have everything I need.
I am full of thankfulness and appreciation.
I believe in myself, I love myself, I am successful.
I am giving from my abundance.
I have nothing worth complaining about.
I am full of love, peace, joy, happiness, faith, and hope.
I believe that everything in my life is working out for good.

· · · · · · ·

"I am by nature a dealer in words, and words are the most powerful drug known to humanity."
— Rudyard Kipling - Author of *The Jungle Book* (1865-1936)

When you sit down to the dinner table of life, what are you eating? You wouldn't make your problems the main meal, would you? So don't make the mistake of eating them again and again through your conversations with yourself and others.

When you talk, speak positively about yourself and the people in your life.

Choose to place encouragement and inspiration as the centerpiece on your table. Choose to display the roses, not the wilted flowers. Feast on all the positive things in your life and decide to eat for dessert... happiness, gratitude, and all the fruits of life. Everyone eventually gets to sit down at the dinner table of life and eat the fruit from the seeds they have sown. Sow good thoughts, feelings and words and live a healthy and fruit-full-life.

> "If you believe the doubts in your mind, you won't achieve the dreams in your heart."
> — Marinela Reka - Author of *A Little Whisper*

Your life becomes the words you speak. For what you are saying with your mouth is coming from your heart and mind, expressing what you believe to be your truth. Stop saying, "I wish" and start saying, "I will." Begin saying, "I can" and stop saying, "I can't." Forget about "I was" and embrace the great "I am."

· · · · · · ·

One of my favorite spiritual teachers, Joel Osteen, author of many books including *Break Out!*, instructs us that, "Whatever follows 'I AM,' is going to come looking for you."...

I AM... unworthy, weak, poor, sick, bored, afraid, insecure, cursed, old, fat, untalented, mistrusting, doubtful, discouraged, stupid, ugly, sad, bad, a failure, complaining, unhappy, tired, depressed, blessed, smart, beautiful, grateful, excited, enthusiastic, happy, healthy, special, strong, prosperous, confident, faithful, successful, wealthy, and wise.

WHAT DO YOU SAY TO YOURSELF… ABOUT WHAT YOU DON'T LIKE ABOUT YOURSELF?

I AM _____.

I AM _____.

I AM _____.

I AM _____.

I AM _____.

Now is your opportunity to rewrite your "I AM," by replacing the negative things you wrote with how you would like yourself to be.

I AM _____.

I AM _____.

I AM _____.

I AM _____.

I AM _____.

· · · · · · ·

"Until one is committed, there is hesitancy, the chance to draw back, always ineffectiveness. There is one elementary truth, that the moment one definitely commits oneself, then providence moves too."
— William Murray - 19th Century Scottish Writer

Make a choice every morning to start your day with encouraging words of heart-felt gratitude by saying, "I am blessed, healthy, and highly favored. Great things are going to happen to me today in every way. Everyone I come in contact with will be positively touched by me. I am loving and giving. With a positive attitude, I speak goodness into all people, places, and things."

"Your echo depends on you. If you scream good things, the world will give it back. If you scream bad things, the world will give it back. Even if someone says things badly about you, speak well about them. Change your heart, to change the world."
— Shams-i Tabrizi - Author of *Me and Rumi*

· · · · · · ·

LIFE IS AN ECHO

A son and his father are walking in the mountains when suddenly the son falls, hurts himself, and screams… "Aahhh." To his surprise, he hears his own voice repeating somewhere in the mountain… "Aahhh."

He looks to his father and asks, "What's going on?" The father smiles and says, "My son, pay attention." And then he screams to the mountain, "I admire you!" The voice answers, "I admire you!" Again the man screams, "You are a champion!" The voice answers, "You are a champion."

The boy is surprised, but he does not understand. Then the father explains, "People call this an echo, but really this is life. It gives you back everything you say or do. Our life is simply a reflection of our actions."

· · · · · · ·

252

THE LAW OF REAPING AND SOWING SAYS... If you want more love, create more love in your heart. In order to be happier, you must be willing to help others be happy. If you want more abundance in your life, then give in all ways to all things. To be blessed, you need to be a blessing to others. If you want corn, then plant corn seeds. If you want flowers, plant flower seeds. This relationship applies to everything, in all aspects of life. Life will give you back everything you have given to it... just like an echo.

"Every little thing you do adds up, and before you know it, you've created your life. And how you create your life ripples out and affects everyone and everything that crosses your path, known or unknown to you."
— Kathy Freston - Author of *Quantum Wellness*

IT'S ALL ABOUT PERSPECTIVE... Some say life is hard, while others say it's a gift. Others say life is a blessing, while some say it's a curse! Some say life isn't fair, while others say life is full of abundance. Others say life sucks, while some say, "Life is great and getting better every day." A fresh perspective about life turns the ordinary into the extraordinary.

"We either make ourselves miserable or we make ourselves strong. The amount of work is the same."
— Carlos Castaneda - Author of *The Teachings of Don Juan*
(1925-1998)

Life can be seen as a living hell, or a heaven on earth. A palace can become a prison, and prosperity can become a form of poverty. We're all challenged by these counter perspectives every single day! Are you going through life or learning through life?

> "Looking back on my life, I had other times when I should have woken up but didn't. This time I really did and made many changes in the way I live my life. The result is a more fulfilling life and a deeper perspective."
>
> — Arianna Huffington - Author of *Thrive*

Some years ago, I began to realize that the words that came out of my mouth were coming from my soul. That my subconscious was listening to what my conscious mind was saying to itself when I spoke. Since words are things, they have a major impact on our attitudes, feelings, and actions. Words are the soul speaking to the world, expressing its emotional, mental, physical, and spiritual condition.

Another thing I began to notice was when I asked people, "How are you doing?" some people answered, "I'm okay" even when I could tell they weren't doing so good! This made me realize I did the same thing and I wasn't being authentic and honest with myself or truthful to others. By saying, "I'm fine," I wasn't declaring anything powerful or life-changing within my chosen words. How many times throughout the day do you hear people say, "Have a great day"… yet how many of them actually do?

Words have a powerful influence on both the speaker and the listener. Now when someone greets me and asks me how I'm doing, I say… "Things are great"… "Life is good"… "Everything is awesome!" When I began to become more aware of words, my feelings and attitude about life gradually changed. Words are powerful things, and when we speak them, they manifest into our physical reality. As a person speaks from his or her heart, so he or she is.

· · · · · · ·

THE POWER OF WORDS

A group of frogs was traveling through the woods, and two of the frogs fell into a deep pit. All the other frogs gathered around the pit, and when they saw how deep the pit was, they told the two frogs that they were as good as dead!

The two frogs ignored the comments and tried to jump up and out of the pit with all of their might. The other frogs kept telling them to stop, that it was hopeless. Finally, one of the frogs took heed to what the other frogs were saying and gave up. He fell down and died.

The other frog continued to jump as hard as he could. Once again, the crowd of frogs yelled at him to stop the pain and just die. He jumped even harder and finally made it out. When he got out, the other frogs said, "Didn't you hear us?" The frog explained to them that he was deaf. He thought they were encouraging him the entire time.

This story teaches us that an encouraging word to someone who is down, can lift a person up and help him or her make it through the day. A destructive word to someone who is down, can be what it takes to kill him. Speak life to those who cross your path. An encouraging word can go such a long way.

· · · · · · ·

THE TONGUE HAS NO BONES… yet it is strong enough to break a heart and destroy someone's life. There have been too many times in my life when I would have loved to be able to reel back in the words that were cast from my mouth! Either in anger, emotional pain, or frustration, I have said things I wished I could have taken back! Even when I apologized and said I didn't mean what I said, the damage was already done!

The tongue is like a two-edged sword; it cuts both ways. It can be used to bless or curse, encourage or destroy, express love or hatred, to heal or to hurt. It's all about the words you choose to use or abuse, within the attitude and tone of your voice. It isn't what goes into our mouth that harms us the most; it's what comes out of the mouth that causes the greatest injuries.

The tongue weighs very little, yet so many people aren't strong enough to hold it! Many people have perfectly good eyes, yet they do not see. Some people speak many words, but say nothing at all.

> "Death and life are in the power of the tongue and they
> that love it, shall eat the fruit thereof."
> — The Bible - *Proverbs 18:21*

So be careful with your words. Think before you speak. Keep your words nice and sweet because you never know which ones you'll have to eat. The words we speak can be thrown like stones, or given as a gift of love. Always say what you mean and mean what you say. Be a person of your word. Words are cheap if you speak them carelessly or good as gold when you make each valuable word count.

TELLING THE TRUTH OR A LIE... Just imagine if it were totally impossible for human beings to lie! Animals don't lie. New born babies can't lie. We are taught and conditioned to lie in order to protect ourselves or to get what we want. Just imagine if when our politicians lied, they would be instantly thrown out of office! Imagine if when you lied, your entire body would shut down and you couldn't function again until you told the truth.

In a study published in *Psychology Today*, which surveyed 1,000 Americans, the research concluded that men lie 1.93 times per day and women lie 1.39 times daily. By the time an average man is fifty years old, he has told over 50,000 lies and a woman more than 30,000. Of course, the figures would be much higher for politicians and lawyers!

Envision a world in which there was no other possibility except "telling the truth." Wow... that would create a different reality than we see on TV and in the newspapers! The world is so full of deception, lying, and manipulating. No matter what the consequences are, choose to tell the truth and it will always keep things very, very real.

"When you tell a lie, you steal someone's right to the truth."
— Khaled Hosseini - Author of *The Kite Runner*

· · · · · · ·

I wrote, sang, and recorded my original song "People, Places, Friends of Mine" on my independent recording label "Robsongs." Here are a few of the lyrics that reflect on making a shift in your life...

People, places, friends of mine,
floating through their space and time.
Will they ever hear their rhythms,
the poetry of life?

Can you hear their voices?
Can you see your choices?
Can you feel what's coming, in your life?

We will come and we will go,
learning things we didn't know.
Reach inside I want to know,
the world that lies within.

· · · · · · ·

Our consciousness, which is the awareness of our thoughts and feelings, creates the type of actions we express into the world around us.

When I'm in Laguna Beach, California, I really enjoy taking a beautiful hike into the pristine Laguna Canyon Wilderness Preserve. In order for one even to think about going on this nature experience, you need to have a burning desire to get in touch with nature and a passion to be one with the environment. You've got to dress for it, drive there in your car, be in good enough shape, and put out the effort with each sweat-filled step up the steep trail.

Yet on the way, some person chose to be eating McDonald's French fries, and when he or she was done, threw the box into the bushes! What was he or she thinking? How can you have a perception of enjoying nature this way? Or is the person so disconnected that, "They know not what they do?"

Common sense may not be as common as you think! Have you ever seen trash thrown away onto the ground, deep into natural places of beauty? It never ceases to amaze me! I have hiked deep into the tropical jungle in Hawaii, and while sitting on a rock in front of an awesome waterfall, I look down and see a beer bottle, a cigarette butt, and litter within the exotic ferns and flowers.

So in order to be the change I want to see in the world, I chose to make a conscious shift by deciding to pick up the trash that someone else mindlessly threw away. This makes me part of the solution and causes a positive effect on the environment and the problems around me. Complaining, judging, getting upset and irritated takes more energy than picking up their garbage, and it makes a beautiful difference in our world.

· · · · · · ·

"From error to error, one discovers the entire truth."
— Sigmund Freud - Famous Psychoanalyst (1856-1939)

The river doesn't have a plan or a dream of becoming the ocean. It does not sit around wondering where it was or where it is going or what the future holds downstream! It just "Is", simply going with the flow of where it was, and will be, while living in the strong current of the moment.

Our spirit, our inner soul, knows what is right and what is wrong and in what direction we should go. The challenge is to hear that still, small voice and listen to what the voice is saying. When we do this, we will find the strength, wisdom, peace, and harmony that transform our lives. If you don't ask yourself the question, you will never become the answer.

• • • • • • •

TODAY... I choose to be happy.
TODAY... I choose to participate in love.
TODAY... I choose to be inspired.
TODAY... I choose to be grateful.

• • • • • • •

"Plant your own garden and decorate your own soul, instead of waiting for someone to bring you flowers."
— Veronica A. Shoffstall - Poet, "After A While"

• • • • • • •

LIFE IS TOO SHORT

Smile until it hurts, Laugh until you cry,
Love like you never have been broken.
Pray with faith, Live in the moment,
Remember the good times and let go of the bad.

Forget the past, Learn from your mistakes,
Be grateful for what you have.
Live and let live, Forgive those who don't deserve it,
Laugh when you can, Apologize when you should,
And let go of what you can't change.

Kiss slowly, Love deeply, Forgive quickly, Take chances,
Give everything you can, And have no regrets.
Because life is too short to be anything but happy!

"Life is too short to wake up with regrets. So love the people
who treat you right, forget about those who don't and believe
everything happens for a reason. Nobody said life would be
easy, they just promised it would most likely be worth it."
— Harvey Mackay - Author of *Dig Your Well Before You're Thirsty*

COURSE FIFTEEN

Being Your Change

Everything changes with or without you! Life has no remote control. So if you want to change the channel and see something different, you have to get out of your easy chair and change it yourself!

The world can change you or you can change your world. We only change when we have to and only when we want to. Yet the experience of living is always changing, and never remains the same. Things don't change; we change. Change is the living process that is lived day by day. Sometimes change happens slowly; other times it strikes like lightning, taking place in a flash!

> "Whatever relationships you have attracted in your life at this moment, are precisely the ones you need in your life at this moment. There is a hidden meaning behind all events, and this hidden meaning is serving your own evolution."
> — Deepak Chopra - Author of *The Seven Spiritual Laws of Success*

IN A MOMENT… a breath, a step, a thought, things can change from good to bad, from worse to better. Gratitude is the act of living inside the appreciation for everything you have in your life, right now. Not what you had in the past. Not what you will receive in the future. All of your true riches are wrapped inside the gift of living in your "Present." You can't start the next chapter if you keep re-reading the last one from your book of life.

CHANGE… is clear, consistent, demonstrated behavior that reflects the definition of change, which is to alter, make different, adjust, modify, revise, reshape, reorganize, replace, rearrange, evolve, and transform.

All I know for sure is that my entire life is contained in this very moment and I have to be present in order to experience it fully. Change is the resurrecting of the soul into the now.

"You cannot change your destination overnight, but you can change your direction overnight. Your life does not get better by chance, it gets better by change."
— Jim Rohn - Author of *My Philosophy for Successful Living* (1930-2009)

The positive and negative experiences you go through change you into who you are today. From the beginning to the end, you are the result of everything you are taught in the courses of going through Life School. When you stop dwelling over your already lived past, it focuses you on the hope of the future. Life is a journey, not a destination. You don't start at the end, otherwise you would miss all of the living and learning experiences.

"Life is what happens while you're busy making other plans."
— John Lennon - The Beatles (1940-1980)

THE KEY TO CHANGE… is letting go of fear. Nobody can go back in time and start a new beginning, yet everyone can start today with making a new ending. You can't change what you refuse to confront. Sometimes it's the smallest decisions that can change your life forever. Ancient Greek philosophy teaches us that all things come into being by the conflict of opposites. Everything changes and nothing remains still in the flow of time. You cannot step twice into the same water, in the same stream. Release the resistance and fear of things being different and allow something new to take its place.

CHANGING MY THINKING...
CHANGES MY FEELINGS...
WHICH CHANGES MY ACTIONS...
WHICH CHANGES MY WORLD.

Worry attracts more of what you don't want, while faith brings more of what you do want. So when you are distressed, cast your eyes toward the heavens, and when a shooting star lights up the dark sky, make a wish and think of all the good things you can be grateful for.

. . . .

YESTERDAY, TODAY AND TOMORROW

There are two days in every week about which we should not worry. Two days which should be kept free from fear and apprehension. One of these days is yesterday, with its mistakes and cares, its faults and blunders, its aches and pains. Yesterday has passed forever beyond our control. All the money in the world cannot bring back yesterday. We can't undo a single act we performed. We can't erase a single word we said. Yesterday is gone beyond recall.

The other day we should not worry about is tomorrow, with its possible adversities, its burdens, its large promise, and perhaps its poor performance. Tomorrow is also beyond our immediate control. Tomorrow's sun will rise, either in splendor or behind a mask of clouds, but it will rise. Until it does, we have no stake in tomorrow, for it is as yet unborn.

This leaves only one day, today. Anyone can fight the battles of just one day. It is only when you and I add the burden of those two awful eternities, yesterday and tomorrow, that we break down. It's not the experience of today that drives us mad. It's the remorse or bitterness for something that happened yesterday or the dread of what tomorrow may bring.

Let us, therefore do our best to live but one day at a time. One today is worth two tomorrows. Eventually one comes to realize that his or her past isn't going to get any better.

· · · · · · ·

"Every change is a type of death, a death to an old way of living or being. To live is to grow, to grow is to change, to change is to die to the old. Divorce, a serious illness, financial disaster, death of a parent, many such an experience feels almost worse than death itself."
— Robert Brumet - Author of *Finding Yourself In Transition*

WE CAN RESIST CHANGE... yet it will occur regardless of whether we want things to change or not! The legendary martial artist and actor, Bruce Lee, suggests that we "Empty the mind, be formless, shapeless like the water. When you put water into a cup, it becomes the cup. If you put water into a bottle, it becomes the bottle." You need to be the change you want to see in your world by changing your inside, which changes your outside.

"The sages do not consider that making no mistakes is a blessing. They believe that the great virtue of a person, lies in their ability to correct their mistakes and continually make a new person of themselves."
— Wang Yangming - Confucian Philosopher (1472–1529)

The skin replaces itself once a month, the stomach lining every five days, the liver every six weeks, and the skeleton every three months. To the naked eye, these organs look the same from moment to moment, but they are always changing through renewing. By the end of this year, 98 percent of the atoms in your body will have been exchanged for new ones.

"You cannot control what happens to you, but you can control your attitude toward what happens to you, and in that, you will be mastering change, rather than allowing it to master you."
— Brian Tracy - Author of *Change Your Thinking, Change Your Life*

You can't have inspired personal growth and change without continued mistakes, successes, failure, loss, and renewal. For this is the way of the world we're all born into and live through.

• • • • • • •

HOW DO YOU KNOW?

Many years ago, in a poor village, there lived a peasant with his only son. His only material goods, besides the land and his little straw hut, was a horse he had inherited from his father. One good day, the horse ran away, leaving the man without a horse to till the land. His neighbors, who respected him for his honesty and diligence, came to his home to let him know how much they regretted what happened. He thanked them for their visit, but asked, "How would you know that what has happened is a misfortune in my life?"

Somebody commented in a low voice to a friend, "He doesn't want to accept reality! Let him think what he wants, as long as he doesn't get sad because of what has happened." And the neighbors went away, trying to be in agreement with what they had heard.

A week later, his horse came back to the stable, but he was not alone. He brought with him a beautiful mare as company. After hearing about this, the inhabitants of the village became overjoyed, because only now did they understand the answer the man had given them. They all returned to the peasant's home to congratulate him for his good luck. "Before you had just one horse; now you have two. Congratulations," they all said.

"Thank you very much for your visit and your sincerity," answered the peasant. "But how do you know that what has happened to me is a blessing in my life?" Confused, and thinking the man was turning insane, the neighbors walked away, commenting while walking home, "Is it possible that this man does not understand that God sent him a gift?"

A month passed by, when the peasant's son decided to tame the mare. But the horse jumped in an unexpected way, and the boy fell and broke his leg. The neighbors came back to the peasant's home, bringing with them presents for the wounded youth. The mayor of town gave his condolences to the father, saying that all were very sad because of what had happened. The father thanked them all for their caring visit and then he asked, "How can you know if what happened has been a misfortune in my life?"

This statement left everyone astonished, since there was no doubt that an accident like what had happened to his only son was a true tragedy. While leaving the peasant's home, they commented among themselves, "He really is becoming crazy! His only son may end up lame forever and he still has doubts about whether or not what has happened is a tragedy!"

Several months went by and war was declared on their nation. The generals went through the country looking for healthy boys to be sent to the battle-front to fight and die for their country. When they arrived at the village, they drafted all the young men except the peasant's son, who was still in a cast for his broken leg. None of the boys returned home alive!

The father's son recovered, the two horses produced babies that were sold at the local market for very good money, and life was better than it had ever been. The peasant went to visit his neighbors to console and help them, since they had shown so much concern and compassion toward him in the past.

When any of them complained, the peasant father would always say, "How do you know if this is a tragedy?" If somebody was too happy, he would ask them, "How do you know if this is a blessing?" Finally, the men and women of that village understood, "That beyond appearances, the changes in life will always have other meanings and we seldom know the real reasons things happen the way they do for the time being!"

. . . .

"When one door to happiness closes, another opens. But often we look so long at the closed door, that we do not see the one which has opened for us."
— Helen Keller - Deaf and Blind Author of *Out of The Dark* (1880-1968)

You may be riding on the right bus, yet sitting in the wrong seat and going in the wrong direction. You can't change where you have been or what you've done. Yet you can use it to change who you are, where you are going, and what you're doing now. You will remain the same, until the pain of remaining the same becomes greater than the pain of making a change.

Billionaire and co-founder of Apple Computers, Steve Jobs, said this about change… "I look into the mirror every morning and ask myself, 'If today were the last day of my life, would I want to do what I am about to do today?' And whenever the answer has been 'No' for too many days in a row, I know I need to change something."

You can't change something until you acknowledge it, define it, and get fully in touch with what you know in your heart you need to change! You must embrace and except it "As is." Giving your focus and total attention to how it really is gives you the power and awareness to awaken to the solutions and answers for changing it.

"I guess it's hard for some people who are so used to things the way they are, even if they're bad, to change, because I guess they kinda give up. And when they do, everybody kinda loses."
— *Pay It Forward* movie 2000

There is a cost for the things in life that are worth the most, and it's through this payment process that we find our greatest treasures. We can all afford to pay the price, yet it's more a matter of our willingness or unwillingness to spend the emotional, mental, and physical currency!

"Only those who can see the invisible, can achieve the impossible. The belief in your vision is the key to creating your own destiny!"
— Patrick Snow - Author of *Creating Your Own Destiny*

Love, peace, joy, happiness, faith, patience, goodness, self-control, kindness, and gratitude, are just some of the fruits from the tree of inspired change. If you don't like what you're eating from the "Menu of Life," decide to order something different that will taste better! Higher consciousness is not a destination; it is an insightful state of mind, being, and doing.

Life has no script or screenplay to follow. You are the actor and this world of inspiration is your stage. Change happens when you think differently than you have always thought, while acting differently than you have always acted. New thoughts and actions are necessary in order to see a change in yourself. You must think and act your new life into existence by being transformed by the renewing of your mind and taking the next right action.

As long as you have hope, faith, and love, your situation will always have the power and possibilities for change. You must be willing to do whatever it takes to have in your life, the things you want to experience as change. Always remember, the person who removes a mountain begins by carrying away a few small stones.

Too often, crisis precedes change. Yet we sometimes try so hard to do it our way, even when our way isn't working. Ultimately, even the wrong way becomes the right way when we change our course and go in the corrected direction. The road leading down your life of change is always under construction. Once you choose a new direction, there will always be a pathway to take you there.

One of the most transforming moments in life is when you find the courage to let go of the things you can't change… "God, grant me the serenity to accept the things I cannot change, the courage to change the things I can, and the wisdom to know the difference."

In their book, *Habits Die Hard,* John J. Murphy and Mac Anderson ask you to take a little test that displays the power of our habits. So please pause for a minute, put this book on your lap, and… "Cross your arms as you normally would, and look down to see which one is on top. About half of you will have your right arm on top and the other half will have their left on top. Now, cross your arms again, but this time put the opposite arm on top. It feels extremely weird, doesn't it! If you were to challenge yourself to cross your arms the 'wrong way' for the rest of your life, could you do it? Probably! Would it be difficult? You bet it would! The real key to success is replacing destructive habits with successful habits."

"Be patient with yourself. Self-growth is tender, it's holy ground. There is no greater investment."
— Stephen Covey - Author of *The 8th Habit* (1932-2012)

. . . .

A CALL TO ACTION

DECIDE RIGHT NOW... to be brutally honest with yourself and to let go of what isn't working in your life. You can't run a successful business without taking an inventory. So if you want to be successful at the business of living, then choose to take an inventory of yourself right now...

ASK YOURSELF... What things would you do differently in your life, if you were given the opportunity to change them?

1. _____.

2. _____.

3. _____.

4. _____.

5. _____.

"Some changes look negative on the surface, yet you will soon
realize that space is being created in your life for
something new to emerge."
— Eckhart Tolle - Author of *Stillness Speaks*

WHAT THINGS HAVE YOU CHANGED IN THE PAST THAT MADE LIFE BETTER?

1. _____.

2. _____.

3. _____.

4. _____.

5. _____.

SO YOU FEEL LIKE YOU MAY NOT BE READY... Doubt
will always kill more dreams than failure ever will. Nobody ever
feels 100 percent ready for change! When a great opportunity
arises, it forces us to grow beyond our comfort zone. This usually means we won't feel totally comfortable at first. So embrace
the discomfort and use it to make yourself comfortable.

WHAT THINGS DO YOU THINK AND FEEL YOU SHOULD CHANGE TODAY?

1. _____.

2. _____.

3. _____.

4. _____.

5. _____.

Someone once said to me, "You don't know, what you don't know, until you know it." It took me a few seconds to process this statement, and then I responded by saying, "Now I know, what I didn't know, because now I know it!"

IF YOU COULD CHANGE ONE CHOICE OR DECISION YOU HAVE MADE IN THE PAST, WHAT WOULD IT BE?

_____

_____

_____

· · · · · · ·

The surf at Honolua Bay on the Hawaiian Island of Maui was much bigger than we had expected! After a long, hard paddle out, my friend Paul took off on a very big wave, wiped out, and broke his surfboard in half! The strong current was pulling him into a place we all dreaded called "The Cave."

I took off on an amazing wave, and after riding it all the way into the inside reef, I paddled toward Paul to see whether he needed my help. I saw he was already bleeding from hitting the coral bottom and was struggling with trying to paddle half of a surfboard. Paul's physical strength and adventurous spirit empowered him to save himself from the perilous rocks and certain injury.

As we paddled back to the beach, he said the fear made him feel alive, and he was having the time of his life! We celebrated that night in Lahaina Town, after he bandaged his wounds and paid the price for breaking a rental board in Hawaii.

Paul shared with me that he wasn't happy with his life and that he had always dreamed of living in Maui. After a few drinks, he continued to open up about how he was afraid to take the risks that come with deciding to make a major change. He had it all: looks, talent, personality, and success. He had more than enough money to take care of his needs and live comfortably anywhere he wanted in the world. He had the capability to make his most passionate dreams come true.

You see, money is meant to give you the ability to carry out the choices you want to make. It gives you the power to change your "wish I could" and "if I only" to "I can afford to" and "I will do it." Paul's dreams were being robbed by his fears as he drank from the bottle of lost and unfulfilled dreams.

You can't be a winner if you're afraid of losing. If you don't take chances, the odds will always be against you! If you have never failed, you have never really lived, and will never learn how to succeed fully at living.

I told Paul he had nothing to lose and everything to gain by making a decision to move to Maui. I advised him to go for it, just like he'd done when he took off on the big wave that snapped his surfboard into two pieces. My advice to him was that no matter what happened, he could always say he'd done it! He would always be better off for doing it, rather than living with the regret for allowing his fear of change to stop him.

276

"You'll seldom experience regret for anything that you've done,
it's what you haven't done that will torment you.
The message therefore is clear. Do it!"
— Dr. Wayne Dyer - Author of *Your Sacred Self*

Paul left paradise and went back home to everything that was comfortable, familiar, and secure. He called me to say his back was killing him, and no matter what the doctors did or how many pain relievers he took, there was very little relief.

From his hospital bed, he answered my questions about his back surgery, yet all he really wanted to talk about was how he wanted to get well again, so he could fulfill his dream of living in Hawaii and riding the waves he so longed to surf again. Paul and I always ended our phone conversations with saying, "Friends for life."

After several weeks of leaving messages on his cell phone, I hadn't heard back from him. When I got home and checked my voicemail, I was shocked to hear his girlfriend's voice telling me... "Paul has passed away!" What do you mean? He can't be gone! He told me he was getting better and we were planning his surfing trip and move to Maui.

Paul never talked about the fact that he was dying. The last time we spoke, it was all about his desire to live the life he had always dreamed of living. He was painfully aware that he was allowing the fear of change to stand in the way of his pursuing a life beyond his great unknown.

"You can't choose how you are going to die or when.
You can only choose how you are going to live."
— Joan Baez - American Folk Singer

What are you thinking and how are you feeling after reading this story? Do you see yourself somewhere within these words? I do! Your life can only be experienced today, not lived in the past or in fear of what might happen in the future. Time is the most precious thing we have. So don't waste it; use it wisely and appreciate every moment. And ask yourself, "Will I live out my dreams, or die with them still inside of me?"

· · · · · · ·

"The moment a person ceases to bemoan their lack of opportunities and resolutely looks their conditions in the face, and resolves to change them, they lay the cornerstone of a solid and honorable success."
— Hamilton Wright Mabie - Author of *Parables of Life* (1846-1916)

We are all attached to some kind of fear we have learned in life. We cannot truly live until we conquer our fears. When a mighty elephant is young, it is chained to an unmovable stake and it soon learns that it can't break free! Then when it grows into a big and powerful adult, it is tied to the same stake with only a rope. The strong steel has been replaced with only weaved fibers, so the elephant has more than enough strength to break the rope and set itself free. Yet it doesn't even try because in the past it was taught that it wasn't powerful enough to do it.

You have to crack the surface in order to let the light in. Until we change our past beliefs toward what we think and feel we can and can't do, we'll always be chained to our old ways of being, thinking, and feeling. What are you still tied to, that if you just had a little faith, you would see that you have all the strength and power you need to set yourself free from it?

We all live in some kind of cage of our own making. Yet some people will remain trapped because it's much easier not to see the bars. People don't know they're stuck until they release themselves with self-awareness. A bird doesn't know it's caged until the day the barred door is opened and it finds the courage to set itself free!

· · · · · · ·

ACTION REQUIRED

Do yourself a big favor and read these words a few times every day... "Right now, I make my decision to break free from these unhealthy emotional chains that bind me and the negative thoughts that imprison me within this jail of my own making. I have spent far too much time looking through the bars of heartache, regret, disappointment, depression, loss, and failure. It's okay to feel afraid and weak, for courage is not the absence of fear, but the strength to triumph over it! I give myself the gift of freedom by loving, forgiving, and transforming myself with the power of God and the help from the people who love me. I am choosing to live my best life today."

· · · · · · ·

279

One day I was looking at the world around me through the eyes and ears of the evening news. The TV is full of violence, killing, war, and destruction. The news always seems to be full of bad news, murders, sex scandals, sickness, disasters, gossip, political corruption, theft, extreme weather, financial problems, and all kinds of mentally and emotionally unhealthy stuff!

I was left with this feeling that there has to be something better than what the media is showing me… somewhere, somehow, and in something. The earth has the potential to be a utopian paradise, yet it seems to be just the opposite! Why is there so much environmental destruction, global warming, chemtrails, starvation, genetically modified organisms in our food, homelessness, pollution, unnecessary death, and out of control greed. The world could be nothing but health, abundant life, truth, honesty, paradise, love, and helping everyone to prosper and have the best life while here on this planet.

The process of seeking a better life and being grateful for what I have in the moment has taught me that if my "Why" is strong enough and I work on it long enough, the "How to do it" will manifest itself into reality. So I grabbed my guitar, wrote, and recorded this song about my feelings that there has to be something better than what I see in this world. When I play and sing these lyrics, I feel a heightened sense of awareness deep inside my soul as I choose to be the change I want to see in my world…

SOMETHING BETTER

I woke up this morning, got in my car, turned on the radio,
The news was all bad, people so sad, living in this world today.

THERE'S GOT TO BE SOMETHING BETTER THAN THIS, I KNOW THAT THERE IS, I BELIEVE THAT THERE IS. THERE'S GOT TO BE SOMETHING BETTER THAN THIS, I KNOW THAT THERE IS, I HOPE THAT THERE IS.

Looking for love in self-satisfaction,
A self-centered life, in this world of temptations.
Take but don't give, I need it to live,
Am I having fun, in this long distance run?

I wake up each morning feeling empty inside,
Working to live, to pay for this ride.
I want to be happy, feel good about life,
But look at this world, caught up in this fight.

THERE'S GOT TO BE SOMETHING BETTER THAN THIS, I KNOW THAT THERE IS, I BELIEVE THAT THERE IS. THERE'S GOT TO BE SOMETHING BETTER THAN THIS, I KNOW WHAT IT IS… FAITH, HOPE, AND LOVE.

· · · · · · ·

In *Life's Little Instruction Book,* by H. Jackson Brown Jr., we are given some very useful guidance on how to live life to its fullest. Here are just a few of them… "Never waste an opportunity to tell someone you love them. Become the most positive and enthusiastic person you know. Be there when people need you. Say, 'Thank you' a lot. Don't expect life to be fair. Don't be afraid to say, 'I made a mistake.' Compliment even small improvements. Keep your promises no matter what."

When I woke up this morning I asked myself, "What is life about?" and I found the answers in my room. The fan said, "Be cool." The ceiling said, "Aim high." The window said, "See the world." The clock said, "Every minute is precious." The mirror said, "Reflect before you act." The door said, "Push hard for your goals." The floor said, "Kneel down, pray, ask for guidance, and be grateful."

"Some people move our souls to dance. They awaken us to
new understanding, with the passing whisper of their wisdom.
Some people make the sky more beautiful to gaze upon. They
stay in our lives for a while, leave footprints in our heart,
and we are never the same."
— Flavia Weedn - Author of *Across The Porch From God*

· · · · · · ·

We are always looking for IT... The IT that will make us happy. The IT that will solve our problems. The IT that will make us rich. The IT that will take care of all our needs. We are always trying just to do IT, feel IT, control IT, possess IT, and be IT, while keeping IT all together. We sometimes fear IT, enjoy IT, hate IT, or love IT.

We are always seeking IT and chasing IT. We want to believe IT, and try not to doubt IT. Of course there are many people and companies that will tell you they have IT and can give IT to you, yet if you want IT, IT isn't free; you will have to pay for IT.

There are many ITs and lots of ways to find IT. There is an IT in spirit, faith, benefit, sincerity, clarity, excitement, humility, gratitude, positive, divinity, commitment, definite, favorite, and prosperity... just to name a few. You see, there are just too many places where IT is, to be able to list them all.

We have an inner hunger to know IT, and learn what IT is and isn't. Only you know what IT is that you need, what IT is you are looking for, and how you will get IT. I think we can all agree that the only thing that is constant is "change." So IT can only be IT for a short period of time, until IT changes or we change IT. And then you take a break from IT, look inside yourself and come to the self-realization that you are "IN-FIN-IT"... Got IT?

· · · · · · ·

FOUR SHORT CLASSES ON CHANGE

<u>Class One</u>

I walk down a street and there's a deep hole in the sidewalk. I fall in. It takes a long time to get out. It's not my fault!

<u>Class Two</u>

I walk down the same street. I fall in the same hole again. It's becoming a habit. I get out immediately. It's my fault.

283

Class Three

I walk down the same street and see the deep hole in the side-walk. I walk around it.

Class Four

I walk down a different street.

"Life is about having to change, taking the moment and making the best of it, without knowing what's going to happen next."
— Gilda Radner - Comedian (1946-1989)

COURSE SIXTEEN

Loving Is Your Test

We are all enrolled in the "School of Life," where we get much of our education through the process of learning to love ourselves and others unconditionally. Love is our greatest teacher and we are her students. All truth is filtered through love. I have found that when you love life, life will love you back.

> "Love isn't separate from the act, it is the act,
> born in the smallest decision to do something."
> —Alex Woodard - Author of *For The Sender*

WHAT IS LOVE?... *The New Oxford American Dictionary* defines love as an intense feeling of deep affection, a romantic or emotional attachment to someone, a great interest or pleasure in something. Love is described with such words as goodwill, friendship, enthusiasm, compassion, charity, adoration, endearment, warmth, fondness, yearning, infatuation, intimacy, desire, tenderness, worship, devotion, appetite, and passion.

> "Love does not insulate others from the harsh realities of living
> in a broken world. Neither can it protect others from the conse-
> quences of their own choices. But love does give broken, hurting
> people a place to find someone who cares for their well-being."
> —Bill Crowder - Author of *Real Love*

Perhaps the best definition I have found for love is in the New Testament Bible: First Corinthians 13:4-8... "Love is patient, love is kind. It does not envy, it does not boast, it is not proud. It does not dishonor others, it is not self-seeking, it is not easily angered, it keeps no record of wrong doings. Love does not delight in evil, but rejoices with the truth. It always protects, always trusts, always hopes, always perseveres. Love never fails. If I have the gift of prophecy and can understand all mysteries and all knowledge, and if I have faith that can move mountains, but have not love, I am nothing! And now these three things remain: Faith, Hope, and Love. And the greatest of these is love."

LOVE is... an action word. It begins as a single drop of water, rising into the heavens, falling upon the earth as heartwarming rain. It turns into a passionate river, becoming an ocean of compassion, sustaining and caring for all living things. You are not meant to wait or search for it. You're meant to give and receive it. Love and happiness are brother and sister and forgiveness and gratitude are their cousins. Actions can be planned, but reactions are spontaneous. They give us a glimpse of what's really in our heart.

"I've learned that people will forget what you said, people will forget what you did, but people will never forget how you made them feel."
— Maya Angelou - Author of *I Know Why the Caged Bird Sings*
(1928-2014)

LOVE is... in a sunrise, a rainbow, a beautiful flower. It's in a delicious meal, a sweet smile, or a thank you. Love is in an unselfish gift, a favor, or a good deed. It's in work, in play, in a kind word, or a caring thought. Love is everywhere, in everything and everyone. To love everything is to forgive everything and to embrace all things as they are. Love liberates the soul.

"Sometimes it feels like there are so many things we can't control, but it's important to remember the things we can, like forgiveness, second chances, fresh starts. Because the one thing that turns the world from a lonely place to a beautiful place, is love. Love in any of its forms. Love gives us hope."
— *New Year's Eve* movie 2011

LOVE is… helping, giving, and sharing. It heals all things. You simply need to open your heart and invite it in. Open up your eyes and see it in all things. Open up your mind and understand how simple love is. Ask for love and you'll receive it. Be it and you'll attract it. Give it away and you'll get more in return.

"Love is a state of being, not a state of feeling. It goes well beyond the realm of the emotions. It's an attitude of kindness towards all creation including one's self, at all times and under all circumstances. Love is the most powerful magnetic force in the universe."
— Carnelian Sage - Author of *The Greatest Manifestation Principle in the World*

LOVE is… life and without love you're not really living. We all need it in order to live a healthy, successful, and prosperous life. Love is the answer to all our questions and the solution to all of our problems. God is love, God is good, God is light, and there is always some good, light, and love in every situation. Even in the darkest of times, love will light the way.

"God is Love, and whenever you reach out in loving kindness, you are expressing God. God is beauty, and whenever you touch the beauty of a flower or a sunset you are touching God. God is the intelligence that creates all and sustains all and binds all together and gives life to all."

— The Peace Pilgrim - *An American Sage Who Walked Her Talk* (1908-1981)

The heart is your-self. The first cell that forms in the human fetus is the heart cell. The heart is formed before the brain, when we are developing inside the womb. When people are asked where their "Self" or "Soul" is located, most people respond by placing their hands over their hearts. The intellectual brain chooses to point to the heart. So begins the life long process of getting out of your head and into your heart.

New scientific research shows that the human heart generates a stronger electrical and magnetic field than the brain. Evidence also shows that the heart is in more control of us than the brain is. The heart sends far more information to the brain than the brain sends to the heart. When your emotions and thoughts are communicating in harmony, your whole being is healthy. When your heart and mind are in dis-harmony, your cells are negatively impacted and you are put into a state of dis-ease. Over two thousand years ago, Jesus said, "As a person thinks in his or her heart, so he or she is."

"What matters is not what is written on the page,
what matters is what's written in the heart."
— Gregory Colbert - Author of *Ashes and Snow*

The heart is the CEO of the body and mind. It's the boss, who is in complete charge and control of our business. The heart is our personality, emotional intellect, the center of our feelings, our true nature, interests, desires, intentions, generosity, sincerity, encouragement, spirit, passion, affection, sympathy, tenderness, understanding, determination, purpose, essence, courage, willpower, fortitude, strength, love, peace of mind, joy, happiness, gratitude, goodness, gentleness, faith, and kindness.

"Depending upon the kind of person you are, you will attract similar energies around you, and others will reciprocate with similar energies. Be kind, compassionate and empathetic so you can attract kindness, compassion and empathy in return. Spread love and enjoy being loved back!"
— Sunetra Basu - Reiki Master

The heart beats an average of seventy times per minute, which is over 100,000 beats every day, more than 35 million times each year and over three billion beats in a lifetime. And within each pumping of the heart, our awareness and heart consciousness is recreated over and over and over again.

"And though the body sleeps, the heart will never rest."
— James Taylor - Song Lyrics, "Shed A Little Light"

For over twenty years, The Institute of HeartMath has been researching the power of positive emotions and the intelligence of the human heart. On its website, I clicked on the most frequently asked questions page and the first question was, "What is Heart Intelligence?" The answer is, "Heart Intelligence is the flow of awareness, understanding and intuition we experience, when the mind and emotions are brought into coherent alignment with the heart."

"The heart does not need to learn how to love. It knows how to love. It never forgets how to love. It is the mind that forgets how to love. It is the mind that needs to remember how to love. And it remembers how to love by practicing the art of compassion."
— Teal Scott - Author of *The Sculptor In The Sky*

A heart without love is like a house without windows. To know love in every breath is to see its miracles on the earth. Love is the tree, we are the branches, and you will always be hungry without this fruit.

"The good person, out of the goodness of their heart, brings forth good things."
— The Bible - *Luke 6:45*

• • • • • • •

A CALL TO ACTION

The more you practice paying more attention to the heart when it's speaking to you, the greater your ability to access this intelligence and guidance will become.

What is your heart intelligence telling you right now?

1. _____.

2. _____.

3. _____.

4. _____.

5. _____.

"Love is like a friendship caught on fire. In the beginning a flame, very pretty, often hot and fierce, but still only light and flickering. As love grows older, our hearts mature and our love becomes as coals, deep-burning and unquenchable."
— Bruce Lee - Martial Arts Actor (1940-1973)

What do you know in your heart of hearts?

1. _____.

2. _____.

3. _____.

4. _____.

5. _____.

· · · · · · ·

"When we silence our brain, quiet our body, and become still enough to feel the beating of our heart, we may be able to remember more profoundly, the thrill of being alive."
— Paul P. Pearsall - Author of *The Heart's Code*

Having fun, laughing, and enjoying life is good for your heart and mind. A study from *The Journal of Behavioral Medicine* found that these actions create health benefits such as a better heart rate, lower blood pressure, and a reduced stress level. It improves sleep, relieves depression, increases energy, promotes happiness, and improves overall health and state of mind.

"Love and happiness are the economy of the heart. They save the expense of anger, the cost of hatred, and the waste of spirits."
— Hannah More - Playwright, *The Search after Happiness* (1745-1833)

LOVING OTHERS... starts with loving yourself. You must love yourself first, before you can love anyone or anything else. Give yourself permission to be unconditionally in love with yourself. You are the most logical source of all the love you need. Self-love is the magnet that attracts all of the other love into your world. See others in the pure spirit of how you would want them to love, accept, forgive, think, and feel about you. Love your outside neighbor as you love your inner self.

"Loving starts with the self. I forgive myself and then I move on. You can sit there forever, lamenting about how bad you've been, feeling guilty until you die, and not one tiny slice of that guilt will do anything to change a single thing in the past."
— Dr. Wayne Dyer - Author of *I Can See Clearly Now*

I AM PERFECTLY IMPERFECT... striving for progress and not perfection. My strength comes from my successes and struggles, my compassion comes from my joy and pain, my wisdom comes from my right and wrong choices, and all that I have which is valuable comes from love.

"I myself am made entirely of flaws, stitched together with good intentions."
— Augusten Burroughs - Author of *This Is How*

THE GOLDEN RULE... can be used to gold plate every thought, word, and deed. "Do to other people only what you would want them to do to you." Or another way to say it is, "Don't do anything to anyone that you wouldn't want him or her to do to you."

"Nothing contributes to the self-image more than being loved by another. When the words, 'I love you' are expressed to you for the first time, your world blossoms, your heart glows with inspiration, confidence, and thoughts of the mountains you can move."
— Robert Conklin - Author of *Be Whole!*

UNCONDITIONAL LOVE... loves those who didn't meet your expectations or let you down. Forgiving Love... forgives those who have hurt and lied to you. Understanding Love... does not seek revenge or try to get even. Compassionate Love... loves those who don't deserve it. Real Love... loves those who don't show you love and appreciation in return.

Loving someone who loves you back is easy. Loving someone you don't like is difficult! It's so much harder to love your enemies, bless those who have done you wrong, and do good for those who hate you! Life has taught me that most of the time, the people who are the hardest to love are the ones who need my love and help the most!

"Any act of kindness, no matter how small, is ever wasted."
— Aesop - Greek Storyteller, *Aesop's Fables* (620BC-564BC)

· · · · · · ·

LOVE IS BLIND

There was a blind girl who hated herself because she was blind. She hated everyone, except her loving boyfriend. He was always there for her. She told her boyfriend, "If I could only see the world, I would marry you."

One day, someone donated a pair of eyes to her. When the bandages came off, she was able to see everything, including her boyfriend. He asked her, "Now that you can see the world, will you marry me?" The girl looked at her boyfriend and saw that he was blind. The sight of his closed eyelids shocked her. She hadn't expected that! The thought of looking at them the rest of her life led her to refuse to marry him.

Her boyfriend left in tears and days later wrote a note to her saying, "Take good care of your eyes my dear... for before they were yours, they were mine!"

· · · · · · ·

The most important thing in life is to learn how to give and receive love. Love is just a word, until people come along and give it meaning and value with their actions. When you do for others, expecting nothing in return, you will get an amazing rate of interest on your investment. If someone doesn't have a smile, it's your job to give him or her one of yours. Without love, we are birds with broken wings, trying to fly and getting nowhere. Inhale love and exhale gratitude.

"There are two basic motivating forces, fear and love. When we are afraid, we pull back from life. When we are in love, we open to all that life has to offer with passion, excitement, and acceptance. If we cannot love ourselves, we cannot fully open to our ability to love others."
— John Lennon - The Beatles (1940-1980)

• • • • • • •

Every year on my birthday, I post a letter to my friends on Facebook. This is what I wrote on my sixtieth…

LOVE IS ALL THERE IS… Today I get the chance to create a brand new start. As I write this, I am reflecting on how this has been a very challenging year for me in so many ways. I got divorced, I lost more money and stuff than I care to calculate, I became depressed, unhealthy and lonely, I had a near-death experience, and moved six times. I moved from Maui, Hawaii to the island of Kauai, back to Maui, to Laguna Beach, California, then to St. Augustine, Florida, back to Laguna Beach, and finally I moved to the west coast of Florida where I bought a home.

Through all of this, I learned to be grateful for the little things in my life, which in time will grow into the big things. All of this forced me to go deeper into myself and to realize that in order for me to love my neighbor, I must love myself first. I began to take a new and sobering look at my unchangeable past, my brand new opportunities, and my eventual passing to the other side.

This helped me to be so grateful for just being alive when so many of my good friends are not! All of this is redefining who I am and what I'm doing with my life. Sometimes I feel lost, yet somehow the challenge of becoming more of me and less of what I was has become the most inspiring experience of my life.

Through all of my challenges and problems, I have received inspired growth, exciting change, and valuable wisdom. As a result, my faith has increased, I have grown closer to God and I'm living within a higher consciousness of love and gratitude.

Unconditionally loving and forgiving myself and others has created such freedom and peace of mind, heart, soul, and spirit. Praying, meditating, and making a mental and written gratitude list became as important to me as air, food, and water. Looking at the positives in my life and seeing what is good and important became my source of healing. Seeing the value in what I still have, instead of being poisoned by all I had lost, was my key to renewed happiness, purpose, and a positive attitude. Everything else was making me sick and unhappy!

For some, what I am sharing may come as a big surprise to you! You might be thinking, "How can this guy who posts all of those inspirational writings and photos on Facebook every day be experiencing this?" You see, I'm just like you. I am both the student and the teacher. I too am going through Life School, while learning from my mistakes, changing from my challenges, being inspired by my experiences, and realizing over and over again, that love is all there really is. And always remember, life will get your attention long enough to give you a good education.

· · · · · · ·

"Character is both developed and revealed by tests, and all of life is a test. You will be tested by major changes, delayed promises, impossible problems, unanswered prayers, undeserved criticism, and even senseless tragedies."
— Rick Warren - Author of *God's Power To Change Your Life*

· · · · · · ·

During her 2009 interview on *Larry King Live*, Suzanne Somers, cancer survivor, actress, and author, shared some deep wisdom she learned from a profound experience she had while in the hospital, fighting for her life.

SOMERS: That's why I wrote this book *Knockout*. Well, I just have to tell you one thing that happened in the hospital because I've had an experience that very few people ever experience. I saw my death! I was in that valley of fear. And one night, I heard a voice. It was so loud that I looked around the room to see if anyone else heard this voice.

KING: What did it say?

SOMERS: "It's not who you are, it's not what you have, it's not what you do, it's only about who you love and who loves you." And I had this moment of the most unbelievable gratitude.

· · · · · · ·

"We can cure physical diseases with medicine, but the only cure for loneliness, despair, and hopelessness is love. There are many in the world who are dying for a piece of bread, but there are many more dying for a little love."
— Mother Teresa - Gallup Poll's "Most Admired Person" (1910-1997)

· · · · · · ·

This story by an unknown author brought tears to my eyes. It contains a message of how love is only true love, when you give it unselfishly, while expecting nothing in return…

UGLY

Everyone in the apartment complex where I lived knew who Ugly was. Ugly was the resident tomcat. Ugly loved three things in this world, fighting, eating garbage, and shall we say, love. The combination of these things, along with a life spent outside, had an effect on Ugly.

To start with, he had only one eye and there was a hole where the other eye should have been. He was missing his ear on the same side. His left foot appeared to have been badly broken at one time, and it had healed at an unnatural angle, making him look like he was always turning the corner. His tail had long ago

298

been lost, leaving only the smallest stub, which he constantly jerked and twitched.

Ugly would have been a dark gray, tabby striped-type, except for the thick, yellow, scabbing sores on his head, neck, and shoulders. Every time someone saw Ugly, there was the same reaction, "That is one ugly cat!"

Children were warned not to touch him. Adults threw rocks at him and hosed him down. They squirted him when he tried to come into their homes, or they shut his paws in the door when he would not leave.

Ugly always had the same reaction. If you turned the hose on him, he would stand there and get soaked until you gave up and quit. If you threw things at him, he curled his lanky body around your feet in forgiveness. When he spied children, he would come running, meowing frantically, and bumping his head against their hands, begging for their love. If someone picked him up, he immediately began suckling on the person's shirt, earrings, or whatever he could find.

One day, Ugly shared his love with the neighbor's Huskies. They did not respond kindly, and Ugly was badly mauled. I heard his yowls from my apartment, and I tried to rush to his aid. But by the time I got to where he was lying, it was apparent Ugly's sad life was almost at an end.

Ugly, in so much pain, suffering and obviously dying, was trying to suckle my ear. I pulled him closer to me as he bumped the palm of my hand with his head. He then turned his one golden eye toward me, and I heard the distinct sound of purring!

Even in his greatest pain, that ugly, battle-scarred cat, wanted only a little affection and perhaps some compassion. At that moment, I thought Ugly was the most beautiful, loving creature I had ever seen. Never once did he try to bite or scratch me, try to get away from me, or struggle in any way. Ugly just looked up at me, completely trusting in me to relieve his pain.

Ugly died in my arms, before I could get him inside. I sat and held him for a long time afterwards, thinking about how one scarred deformed little stray, could so alter my opinion about what it means to have true pureness of spirit and to love so totally and truly.

Ugly taught me more about giving and compassion than a thousand books, lectures, or talk show specials ever could. For that I will always be thankful. He had been scarred on the outside, but I was scarred on the inside. It was time for me to move on, and learn to love truly and deeply. It was time to give my all to those I cared for. Many people want to be richer, more successful, well-liked, and beautiful… but for me, I will always try to be like Ugly.

· · · · · · ·

"Too often we underestimate the power of a touch, a smile, a kind word, a listening ear, an honest compliment, or the smallest act of caring, all of which have the potential to turn a life around."
— Leo Buscaglia - Taught "Love 1A" at USC (1924-1998)

In his book *The Hidden Messages in Water*, Japanese scientist Dr. Masaru Emoto used high-speed photography to document the effects that our thoughts, words, and feelings have on water molecules. He discovered that crystals formed in frozen water revealed changes when specific, concentrated thoughts are directed toward them. He found that water that has been exposed to loving words and positive thoughts produces brilliant, complex, and colorful snowflake patterns. In contrast, water exposed to negative thoughts and harmful words formed incomplete, disfigured ice crystal patterns with dull colors.

The implications of this research create a new awareness of how we can positively impact the world and our personal, mental, emotional, and spiritual health with our words. Since humans and the earth are composed mostly of water, we have the kind of power that affects everything and everyone around us. Dr. Emoto's photographs are amazing and his research reveals the healing power of love.

> "Love is the condition in which the happiness of another person, is essential to your own."
> — Robert A. Heinlein - Author of *Time Enough For Love* (1907-1988)

The same flame that warms your body can also burn your hand! Yet even though I have fried my fingers on the hot stove more than once, I still need to cook my food on the same flame that hurt me! Emotional pain and heartache can make us afraid of loving again because of the fear of being loved and getting hurt one more time. Yet our hearts need love for spiritual nourishment, so we need to keep trying to find a healthy, nutritious, emotional meal within our daily experiences of enlightenment, excitement, healing and believing.

It is a natural defense mechanism to harden your heart for protection. When life throws stones at you, too many of us use them to build a wall around us for safety. When you add another brick, the wall gets taller. If you take a stone away, the wall gets smaller. Add a little love and your life gets better; take your love away and it all gets worse!

"Heartsick, heartbroken, to know love, is to know pain. What could be more common? Even so, each broken heart is so singular, that with it, we probe the divine. Your task is not to look for love, but merely to seek and find all the barriers within yourself, that you have built against it."
— Rumi - Mystic Poet, "Spiritual Couplets" (1207-1273)

Don't write your love on a piece of paper because people can erase it and tear it apart. Don't etch it in stone for time can wear it away and harmful forces can break it. Inscribe your love on the pages of your heart, where nothing can erase, crack, or wear it away. If you love someone, put his or her name in a circle because hearts can be broken, yet circles never end.

"If you enter this world knowing you are loved and you leave this world knowing the same, then everything that happens in between can be dealt with. Let us dream of tomorrow, where we can truly love from the soul, and know love as the ultimate truth at the heart of all creation."
— Michael Jackson - Entertainer, "King of Pop" (1958-2009)

The American sociologist Lewis Muford in his 1951 book, *The Conduct of Life,* teaches… "Without food man can survive for barely thirty days; without water for little more than three days; without air hardly for more than three minutes, but without hope and love, he might destroy himself in an even shorter time."

Mother Teresa, founder of The Missionaries of Charity, expresses her thoughts about love and forgiveness… "It's not how much we do, but how much love we put into the doing. It's not how much we give, but how much love we put into the giving. If we really want to love, we must learn how to forgive. We can do no great things, only small things with great love."

What if the only way you could get anything you needed… food, water, shelter, money, was by giving the same thing to somebody else. For example, if you wanted food, you would have to feed someone who is hungry. If you needed water, you would have to give a drink to someone who is thirsty. If you wanted a better home, you would have to give shelter to the homeless. If you needed more money, you would have to help somebody else financially.

This condition would totally change the world we live in. It would manifest a reaping and sowing, giving and receiving, action and reaction that would create so much love and good that it would be amazing! The good news is that we all have the power and ability to do this. By committing one small, selfless act of love to one person at a time, you can change the world in your own backyard. Love liberates us, forgiveness heals us, and gratitude restores us, with peace, joy, and happiness being the inspired results. Love is the fabric of the universe that holds everything together.

· · · · · · ·

WEALTH, SUCESS, AND LOVE

A man and a woman had been praying for prosperity and their prayers were being answered. They were visited by three angels... Wealth, Success, and Love. Yet they were only allowed to pick one of them to come into their home and bless their lives.

They pondered over their three choices, giving them deep thought and contemplation. He thought, "If we choose Wealth, we can buy our Success and that will bring us Love." She disagreed and thought, "If we choose Success, it will bring us Wealth and we can then afford to be in Love." After they prayed together for guidance, they both agreed to choose Love.

"Which one of you is Love?" asked the couple. "Please come in and fill our home." Love started walking toward the house, and then the other two stood up and followed. Surprised, they asked Wealth and Success, "We were told we could only pick one, so why are you also coming into our home?" They answered, "If you had invited Wealth or Success to come into your home, the other two would have stayed outside. But since you invited Love, where Love goes, we follow. For wherever there is Love, there is also Wealth and Success."

· · · · · · ·

"Love is the fundamental building block of all human relation-ships. Love is the important ingredient in one's search for meaning. Love is a choice you make everyday."
— Dr. Gary Chapman - Author of *The Five Love Languages*

Open your eyes and look within, are you satisfied with the life you're living? This very moment is the time for you to make the decision to think, feel, and act your way into having the quality of life you have always dreamed of. The moment you've been waiting for your entire life is right NOW!

Make your decision to be living in the cool breezes of wisdom and exhale your last lukewarm breath of regret, disappointment, complaining, and unforgiveness. Now is the time to live the life you have always wanted to be living...

It's a new day, a new song,
A fresh chance, to right your wrongs.
A new start, a new beginning,
Where no one loses, everyone's winning.
See the love, open your eyes,
Peace, joy, happiness, God's power inside.
Health, gratitude, and positive thinking,
Prosperity, hope, and heartfelt giving.
It's a new day, a new song,
The Universe is calling, have faith and come along.

We all have flaws and weaknesses, yet with the right mental, emo-tional, and spiritual exercises, we can turn our faults and limita-tions into our greatest strengths. You have been given the awesome power to change a negative into a positive, sadness into happiness, fear into faith, pain into gain, and bad into good. You can turn wrong choices into right learning, not-so-right decisions into greater wisdom, and "hard knocks" into "opportunity knocks."

During your trials and tribulations, your successes and celebrations, you will receive some of your deepest revelations. They will become your most prized possessions, when measured by the knowledge gained toward your life's priceless education.

Raise your hand high in the classroom of life and receive all the lessons your life wants to teach you. Life School is always in session. There is always another class to take and one more lesson to learn in the University of Life.

You are today who, what, and where you are, because of every lesson you have learned and are still learning *In Life School.*
Life is your classroom…
Experience is your teacher…
Loving is your test.

In one glorious moment, you will hear the eternal recess bell, as you graduate from this "School of Life" and move on to a higher place.

THE END
Or is it your new beginning?

Rob Whalley

LAST CALL TO ACTION

Learn from your yesterdays, apply the lessons to your todays, and embrace the hope of your tomorrows. Your whole purpose of living is to be learning, growing, and changing toward your highest good.

While these inspirational truths are still fresh within your heart, mind, and soul… What lessons do you think and feel you have learned from taking the courses In Life School?

1. _____.

2. _____.

3. _____.

4. _____.

5. _____.

> "I will do today what others won't, so I will have
> tomorrow what others don't."
> —John Addison - Film Composer (1920-1998)

What action steps are you taking to further your studies in the lessons of happiness, forgiveness, change, love, gratitude, thinking, and loving?

1. _____.

2. _____.

3. _____.

4. _____.

5. _____.

"If one advances confidently in the direction of one's dreams, and endeavors to live the life which one has imagined, one will meet with a success unexpected in common hours."

— Henry David Thoreau - Author of *Walden* (1817-1862)

What is or will be different in your life as the result of reading these pages and then doing your best to apply what you read inside this book?

1. _____.

2. _____.

3. _____.

4. _____.

5. _____.

ABOUT THE AUTHOR

Rob Whalley is a 6'2", sixty-year-old, Aquarius-Pisces, who was named after his father, Robert. Rob grew up as the third of six children in a small beach town called Point Pleasant Beach, New Jersey. He stuttered as a child until he realized that his mind was going faster than his mouth because he always had so much to say.

Rob took those thoughts and his high dose of creative energy and fueled them into a career in sales & marketing as well as becoming a songwriter with three CDs to his credit.

But first, following high school, he left college to further his education by going on a long international surfing trip that he called "Life School." He has been learning life lessons ever since.

Rob has always lived by the ocean, whether it was in New Jersey, California, Hawaii, Puerto Rico, the Virgin Islands, the Bahamas, or Florida, where he enjoys the great surf, diving, and beautiful beaches.

Whatever obstacles he has faced, from job loss to divorce and everything in between, he has always found the good and the lesson in his life experiences. Rob explains, "We can overcome life's frustrations and obstacles by embracing the education that life has to offer us. That's why I decided to share my story In Life School."

ACKNOWLEDGMENTS

I would like to thank Susan for suggesting that I write this book. Gaylord, for all of his help, support, and encouragement. Beth, for her spiritual guidance. My Facebook friends, for reading my daily posts and inspiring me with their likes, shares, and comments. Patrick, for his patience during his many years of book coaching me. Candy for her encouraging phone calls. Greg, for coming out of my past to be a mentor and friend. Tyler, for his great editing job and for going beyond the call of duty. Shiloh, for her amazing design work on the cover and inside pages of this book. God, for writing this book with me, through me, and in Him. And thank you to everyone else who had anything to do with helping me write and finish this book.

InLifeSchool.com

Where you can buy more books or an ebook, sign up for DAILY INSPIRATIONAL EMAILS and WEBINARS, learn more about FUNDRAISING opportunities selling my book, chat with like-minded In Life School students, write a BOOK REVIEW or TESTIMONIAL, get free gifts, access life-changing information, and find the tools, products, and services you need to LIVE YOUR BEST LIFE TODAY.

OTHER PRODUCTS FOR SALE

MY ORIGINAL MUSIC CDs…

"For You"
"Jesus Paid the Price"
"In Life School Inspirational Songs"

CUSTOM T-SHIRTS

"Life is great and getting better every day."
"Live your best life today."

Or any part of the book that inspired you,
custom-printed on a T-shirt.

FOR ADDITIONAL BOOKS
or an eBOOK

If you want to buy another book for a friend or family member, or if you want to buy a large quantity of books at a volume saving, go to www.InLifeSchool.com or email me at inlifeschool@gmail.com

REFER THIS BOOK TO FRIENDS AND FAMILY...

GO TO: InLifeSchool.com

CLICK ON THE LINK: Refer *In Life School* to your family and friends.

eBOOK download is available for all device formats at www.InLifeSchool.com

BOOK REVIEWS and TESTIMONIALS NEEDED: Go to InLifeSchool.com and Amazon.com. Share with me how my book touched your heart, mind, and soul. Tell me what you liked about the book, why others should read it, and how the inspirational information is helping you live your best life today.

Sign Up For
DAILY INSPIRATIONAL EMAILS
WITH LIFE-CHANGING WISDOM
AND ENCOURAGEMENT

Get your daily dose of inspiration sent to your email inbox or mobile device.

It's FREE and EASY

1. Go to InLifeSchool.com

2. CLICK on *In Life School Daily Inspirations*

3. Enter your name and email address

4. Adjust your Junk-Mail Settings

5. Receive your Daily, Life-Changing Inspirational emails.

6. Then share this complimentary gift with your family and friends by clicking on the share link.

CONTACT ME AT:
InLifeSchool.com
inlifeschool@gmail.com

FACEBOOK and TWITTER

LIKE my *In Life School* Facebook page, where you can meet other people just like yourself who are facing similar challenges, opportunities, problems, and successes: www.facebook.com/InLifeSchool

Follow me on my personal Facebook page:
www.facebook.com/rob.whalley.9

Follow me on TWITTER:
www.twitter.com/InLifeSchool

MEDIA

Invite me to appear on your Radio Program, TV Show, Webcast, Seminar, or publish part of my book inside your Blog, Newsletter, Newspaper, or Magazine.

BOOK RELEASE PARTY HOSTS WANTED

Host a Book Release Party at your home, business, event, or favorite gathering place. If your life has been so touched by my book *In Life School* that you want to sponsor a book signing party, I will come and personally sign books, give an inspirational talk, read from my book, and hold a question and answer period. As a special bonus, I'll sing a few original inspirational songs on my acoustic guitar.

CONTACT ME AT:
InLifeSchool.com
inlifeschool@gmail.com

BOOK CLUBS WANTED

Make my book, *In Life School,* your book of the month and I will include an hour-plus conference call or Skype, where I will discuss the book with your reader group.

FUNDRAISING
SELLING MY BOOK

Sell my book, *In Life School*, to raise funds for your organization. Whether it's Animal Rescue, an Environmental Foundation, Feeding the Hungry, or any other good cause or charity for which you are seeking financial support. I will help you raise the money you need, to help you do what your heart, mind, and soul is telling you to do. I also have music CDs, T-shirts, health products, jewelry, and other products and services to complement your fundraising program. Contact me to find out the details about how your organization can benefit from this Book-Selling Fundraising Program.

CONTACT ME AT:
InLifeSchool.com
inlifeschool@gmail.com

LIFE COACHING
Using *In Life School* as your textbook

I will personally coach you over the phone or Skype,
in the comfort of your home.

Would you like to talk with Rob Whalley, the author of *In Life School*, about your life and how the wisdom, inspiration and guidance inside this book can help you put it into a more positve and loving perspective?

Do you need help, encouragement, and support applying the information and lessons you have learned through reading *In Life School*?

Do you have some questions or would you like to go beyond the book by learning more about Love, Forgiveness, Gratitude, Happiness, Positive Attitude, Taking Action, and Change?

I would love to be your one-on-one coach and mentor, helping you study the "how to" courses inside my book *In Life School*.

LIFE COACHING WILL HELP YOU TEACH YOURSELF HOW TO:

* ★ Begin making life your classroom, experience your teacher, and love the reason for passing your day-to-day tests.

* Use your life experiences to grow, change, and prosper.

* Turn problems into possibilities and stormy days into good days.

* Move from tragedy, loss, and failure into prosperity, success, and a better life.

* Think your best thoughts, take inspired action, and celebrate your life.

* Create your positive attitude, "Life is great and getting better every day."

* Graduate into living the life you have always dreamed you could.

For more information about personal Life School Coaching, or to schedule your no obligation, complimentary, 15-minute life coaching consultation by phone or Skype, go to InLifeSchool.com and send me an email at inlifeschool@gmail.com and turn your desire to live your best life today into an inspired reality.

CONTACT ME AT:
InLifeSchool.com
inlifeschool@gmail.com

BOOK COACHING
Best-Selling Author Program

As a published author, I can help you achieve
your book publishing, sales and marketing goals.

Do you wish to fulfill your personal dream of writing the book that is inside of you?

Let me help you start, finish, and publish the book of your dreams. I will save you time, and money by helping you avoid the trial and error process.

Use your book as a lead-generating tool to promote your business and get more clients.

I was once where you are. I was overwhelmed by the process and the challenges of book writing and self-publishing. As your book coach, I will be answering your questions, and providing you with the resources and solutions that will contribute to your book writing success. Let me help you simplify the process by being your coach and mentor, who will take you from wanting to write a book to being a published best-selling author.

YOU WILL LEARN HOW TO:

* Write a compelling title, great subtitles, and eye-catching header.

* Create an outline, contents page, and highly informative book content.

* Write your best first chapter and then have it professionally edited.

* Accomplish your final editing, proofreading, front and back book cover design, interior page design, printing, sales, promotion, and marketing.

With this goal in mind, I hope you will contact me to schedule a no obligation, complimentary consultation to answer all your questions about one-on-one book coaching, self-publishing, book-marketing, and how to become a best-selling author.

For more information go to InLifeSchool.com or send me an email at inlifeschool@gmail.com requesting your free 15-minute book coaching consultation by phone or Skype, and turn your desire to write your book into a powerful reality.

CONTACT ME AT:
InLifeSchool.com
inlifeschool@gmail.com

INSPIRATIONAL SPEAKING WORKSHOPS and WEBINARS

My book is my speech
and my speech is my book.

Invite me to speak about the subjects and courses in my book *IN LIFE SCHOOL* for your business, event, seminar, association, club, or webinar.

Book me, Rob Whalley, to speak at your next event. Whether your audience is 10, 100, or thousands, I will deliver a tailor-made message of inspiration based on my book, *In Life School* for your meeting, conference, training, or classroom.

SPEAKING TOPICS INCLUDE:

* ✸ Embracing and achieving positive change and progress.

* ✸ Taking action, making a shift, being your best person today.

* ✸ Becoming a self-inspired leader of your own world.

* ✸ Positive attitude, better thinking, and healthier emotions.

* ✸ Happiness, Forgiveness, Gratitude, Love, Prosperity, Change, Transformation.

* Celebrating your life, increasing self-worth, self-esteem, and self-awareness.

* Using your experiences as your teacher and life as your classroom.

* Learning the lessons your life wants to teach you.

* Turning problems into possibilities, while making it through life's storms.

* Transforming your life by the renewing of your mind and heart.

CONTACT ME AT:
InLifeSchool.com
inlifeschool@gmail.com

LIFE SCHOOL CLASSES

in your home or business.

Start a weekly or bi-monthly small group-gathering with my *In Life School* book as your guide, manual, and textbook, and I will personally call in by phone or Skype to be part of your learning experience.

AFFILIATE MARKETING COMPANIES ADVERTISING * JOINT VENTURES

AFFILIATE MARKETING COMPANIES WANTED…
I am looking for products to sell on my website InLifeSchool.com and to use as fundraisers.

ADVERTISE YOUR BUSINESS in my next book edition and on InLifeSchool.com

INCREASE YOUR COMPANY'S BRAND by printing your own private edition of *In Life School* with your company name, logo, introduction, testimonials, and foreword. Give them to your clients, associates, and future customers.

CONTACT ME AT:
InLifeSchool.com
inlifeschool@gmail.com